Workshop on Textual Entailment 2011

(TextInfer 2011)

Held at EMNLP 2011

Edinburgh, Scotland, United Kingdom
30 July 2011

ISBN: 978-1-61839-244-2

Printed from e-media with permission by:

Curran Associates, Inc.
57 Morehouse Lane
Red Hook, NY 12571

Some format issues inherent in the e-media version may also appear in this print version.

Printed by Curran Associates, Inc. (2011)

For permission requests, please contact the Association for Computational Linguistics at the address below.

Association for Computational Linguistics
209 N. Eighth Street
Stroudsburg, Pennsylvania 18360

Phone: 1-570-476-8006
Fax: 1-570-476-0860

acl@aclweb.org

Additional copies of this publication are available from:

Curran Associates, Inc.
57 Morehouse Lane
Red Hook, NY 12571 USA
Phone: 845-758-0400
Fax: 845-758-2634
Email: curran@proceedings.com
Web: www.proceedings.com

Introduction

Textual inference and paraphrase have attracted a significant amount of attention in recent years. Many NLP tasks, including question answering, information extraction, and text summarization, can be mapped at least partially onto the recognition of textual entailments and the detection of semantic equivalence between texts. Robust and accurate algorithms and resources for inference and paraphrasing can be beneficial for a broad range of NLP applications, and have stimulated research in the area of applied semantics over the last years.

The success of the Recognizing Textual Entailment challenges and the high participation in previous workshops on textual inference and paraphrases – *Empirical Modeling of Semantic Equivalence and Entailment* (ACL 2005), *Textual Entailment and Paraphrasing* (ACL/PASCAL 2007), and *TextInfer 2009* (ACL) – show that there is substantial interest in the area among the research community.

TextInfer 2011 follows these workshops and aims to provide a common forum for researchers to discuss and compare novel ideas, models and tools for textual inference and paraphrasing. One particular goal is to broaden the workshop to invite both theoretical and applied research contributions on the joint topic of "inference." We aim to bring together empirical approaches, which have tended to dominate previous textual entailment events, with formal approaches to inference, which are more often presented at events like ICoS or IWCS. We feel that the time is ripe for researchers from both groups to join for this event, with the goal of establishing a discussion on how the two approaches relate to one another, and how to define interfaces between the two methodologies.

We would like to thank all the people that made this event possible: the authors of submitted papers, the reviewers, and the participants.

Enjoy the workshop!

The workshop organizers,

Peter Clark, Vulcan Inc.
Ido Dagan, Bar-Ilan University
Katrin Erk, University of Texas at Austin
Sebastian Pado, Heidelberg University (Program Co-chair)
Stefan Thater, Saarland University (Program Co-chair)
Fabio Massimo Zanzotto, University of Rome "Tor Vergata"

Organizers:

Peter Clark, Vulcan Inc.
Ido Dagan, Bar-Ilan University
Katrin Erk, University of Texas at Austin
Sebastian Pado, Heidelberg University (Program Co-chair)
Stefan Thater, Saarland University (Program Co-chair)
Fabio Massimo Zanzotto, University of Rome "Tor Vergata"

Program Committee:

Richard Bergmair, University of Cambridge (UK)
Johan Bos, University of Groningen (Netherlands)
Aljoscha Burchardt, DFKI (Germany)
Chris Callison-Burch, John Hopkins University (USA)
Phillip Cimiano, Bielefeld University (Germany)
David Clausen, Stanford University (USA)
Ann Copestake, Cambridge University (UK)
Kees van Deemter, Aberdeen University (UK)
Bill Dolan, Microsoft Research (USA)
Mark Dras, Macquarie University (Australia)
Markus Egg, HU Berlin (Germany)
Anette Frank, Heidelberg University (Germany)
Claire Gardent, LORIA (France)
Andy Hickl, Extractiv/Swingly (USA)
Graeme Hirst, University of Toronto (Canada)
Jerry Hobbs, USC/ISI (USA)
Kentaro Inui Tohoku University (Japan)
Hans-Ulrich Krieger, DFKI (Germany)
Piroska Lendvai, Hungarian Academy of Sciences (Hungary)
Bill MacCartney, Google (USA)
Bernardo Magnini, Fondazione Bruno Kessler (Italy)
Marie-Catherine de Marneffe, Stanford University (USA)
Erwin Marsi, NTNU (Norway)
Yashar Mehdad, University of Trento (Italy)
Detmar Meurers, Tuebingen University (Germany)
Shachar Mirkin, Bar-Ilan University (Israel)
Michael Mohler, University of North Texas (USA)
Dan Moldovan, University of Texas at Dallas (USA)
Robero Navigli, University of Rome (Italy)
Patrick Pantel, Microsoft Research (USA)
Marco Pennacchiotti, Yahoo! (USA)
Ian Pratt-Hartmann, Manchester University (UK)

Dan Roth, University of Illinois at Urbana-Champaign (USA)
Satoshi Sato, Nagoya University (Japan)
Satoshi Sekine, New York University (USA)
Idan Szpektor, Yahoo! (USA)
Ivan Titov, Saarland University (Germany)
Antonio Toral, Dublin City University (Ireland)
Kentaro Torisawa, NICT (Japan)
Annie Zaenen, PARC (USA)

Invited Speaker:

Bill Dolan, Microsoft Research (USA)

Table of Contents

Workshop Program

Saturday, July 30, 2011

8:45–9:00 Opening Remarks

9:00–10:00 Invited Talk by Bill Dolan: "Broad-domain Paraphrasing"

10:00–10:30 *Evaluating Answers to Reading Comprehension Questions in Context: Results for German and the Role of Information Structure*
Detmar Meurers, Ramon Ziai, Niels Ott and Janina Kopp

10:30–11:00 Coffee break

11:00–11:30 *Towards a Probabilistic Model for Lexical Entailment*
Eyal Shnarch, Jacob Goldberger and Ido Dagan

11:30–12:00 *Classification-based Contextual Preferences*
Shachar Mirkin, Ido Dagan, Lili Kotlerman and Idan Szpektor

12:00–12:20 *Is it Worth Submitting this Run? Assess your RTE System with a Good Sparring Partner*
Milen Kouylekov, Yashar Mehdad and Matteo Negri

12:20–12:40 *Diversity-aware Evaluation for Paraphrase Patterns*
Hideki Shima and Teruko Mitamura

12:40–14:20 Lunch

14:20–14:50 *Representing and resolving ambiguities in ontology-based question answering*
Christina Unger and Philipp Cimiano

14:50–15:20 *Strings over intervals*
Tim Fernando

15:20–15:40 *Discovering Commonsense Entailment Rules Implicit in Sentences*
Jonathan Gordon and Lenhart Schubert

15:40–16:10 Coffee break

Saturday, July 30, 2011 (continued)

16:10–17:00 Final Panel and Discussion

Evaluating Answers to Reading Comprehension Questions in Context: Results for German and the Role of Information Structure

Detmar Meurers **Ramon Ziai** **Niels Ott** **Janina Kopp**
Seminar für Sprachwissenschaft / SFB 833
Universität Tübingen
Wilhelmstraße 19 / Nauklerstraße 35
72074 Tübingen, Germany
{dm,rziai,nott,jkopp}@sfs.uni-tuebingen.de

Abstract

Reading comprehension activities are an authentic task including a rich, language-based context, which makes them an interesting real-life challenge for research into automatic content analysis. For textual entailment research, content assessment of reading comprehension exercises provides an interesting opportunity for extrinsic, real-purpose evaluation, which also supports the integration of context and task information into the analysis.

In this paper, we discuss the first results for content assessment of reading comprehension activities for German and present results which are competitive with the current state of the art for English. Diving deeper into the results, we provide an analysis in terms of the different question types and the ways in which the information asked for is encoded in the text.

We then turn to analyzing the role of the question and argue that the surface-based account of information that is given in the question should be replaced with a more sophisticated, linguistically informed analysis of the information structuring of the answer in the context of the question that it is a response to.

1 Introduction

Reading comprehension exercises offer a real-life challenge for the automatic analysis of meaning. Given a text and a question, the content assessment task is to determine whether the answer given to a reading comprehension question actually answers the question or not. Such reading comprehension exercises are a common activity in foreign language teaching, making it possible to use activities which are authentic and for which the language teachers provide the gold standard judgements.

Apart from the availability of authentic exercises and independently motivated gold standard judgements, there are two further reasons for putting reading comprehension tasks into the spotlight for automatic meaning analysis. Firstly, such activities include a text as an explicit context on the basis of which the questions are asked. Secondly, answers to reading comprehension questions in foreign language teaching typically are between a couple of words and several sentences in length – too short to rely purely on the distribution of lexical material (as, e.g., in LSA, Landauer et al., 1998). The answers also exhibit a significant variation in form, including a high number of form errors, which makes it necessary to develop an approach which is robust enough to determine meaning correspondences in the presence of errors yet flexible enough to support the rich variation in form which language offers for expressing related meanings.

There is relatively little research on content assessment for reading comprehension tasks and it so far has focused exclusively on English, including both reading comprehension questions answered by native speakers (Leacock and Chodorow, 2003; Nielsen et al., 2009) and by language learners (Bailey and Meurers, 2008). The task is related to the increasingly popular strand of research on Recognizing Textual Entailment (RTE, Dagan et al., 2009) and the Answer Validation Exercise (AVE, Rodrigo et al., 2009), which both have also generally targeted English.

The RTE challenge abstracts away from concrete tasks to emphasize the generic semantic inference component and it has significantly advanced the field under this perspective. At the same time, an investigation of the role of the context under which an inference holds requires concrete tasks, for which content assessment of reading comprehension tasks seems particularly well-suited. Borrowing the terminology Spärck Jones (2007) coined in the context of evaluating automatic summarization systems, one can say that we pursue an extrinsic, full-purpose evaluation of aspects of textual inference. The content assessment task provides two distinct opportunities to investigate textual entailment: On the one hand, one can conceptualize it as a textual inference task of deciding whether a given text T supports a particular student answer H. On the other hand, if target answers are provided by the teachers, the task can be seen as a special bi-directional case of textual entailment, namely a paraphrase recognition task comparing the student answers to the teacher target answers. In this paper, we focus on this second approach.

The aim of this paper is twofold. On the one hand, we want to present the first content assessment approach for reading comprehension activities focusing on German. In the discussion of the results, we will highlight the impact of the question types and the way in which the information asked for is encoded in the text. On the other hand, we want to discuss the importance of the explicit language-based context and how an analysis of the question and the way a text encodes the information being asked for can help advance research on automatic content assessment. Overall, the paper can be understood as a step in the long-term agenda of exploring the role and impact of the task and the context on the automatic analysis and interpretation of natural language.

2 Data

The experiments described in this paper are based on the Corpus of Reading comprehension Exercises in German (CREG), which is being collected in collaboration with two large German programs in the US, at Kansas University (Prof. Nina Vyatkina) and at The Ohio State University (Prof. Kathryn Corl). German teachers are using the WEb-based Learner COrpus MachinE (WELCOME, Meurers et al., 2010) interface to enter the regular, authentic reading comprehension exercises used in class, which are thereby submitted to a central corpus repository. These exercises consist of texts, questions, target answers, and corresponding student answers. Each student answer is transcribed from the hand-written submission by two independent annotators. These two annotators then assess the contents of the answers with respect to meaning: Did the student provide a meaningful answer to the question? In this binary content assessment one thus distinguishes answers which are appropriate from those which are inappropriate in terms of meaning, independent of whether the answers are grammatically well-formed or not.

From the collected data, we selected an even distribution of unique appropriate and inappropriate student answers in order to obtain a 50% random baseline for our system. Table 1 lists how many questions, target answers and student answers each of the two data sets contains. The data used for this paper is made freely available upon request under a standard Creative Commons by-nc-sa licence.[1]

	KU data set	OSU data set
Target Answers	136	87
Questions	117	60
Student Answers	**610**	**422**
# of Students	141	175
avg. Token #	9.71	15.00

Table 1: The reading comprehension data sets used

3 Approach

Our work builds on the English content assessment approach of Bailey and Meurers (2008), who propose a Content Assessment Module (CAM) which automatically compares student answers to target responses specified by foreign language teachers. As a first step we reimplemented this approach for English in a system we called CoMiC (Comparing Meaning in Context) which is discussed in Meurers et al. (2011). This reimplementation was then adapted for German, resulting in the CoMiC-DE system presented in this paper.

The comparison of student answers and target answer is based on an alignment of tokens, chunks, and

[1] http://creativecommons.org/licenses/by-nc-sa/3.0/

dependency triples between the student and the target answer at different levels of abstraction. Figure 1 shows a simple example including token-level and chunk-level alignments between the target answer (TA) and the student answer (SA).

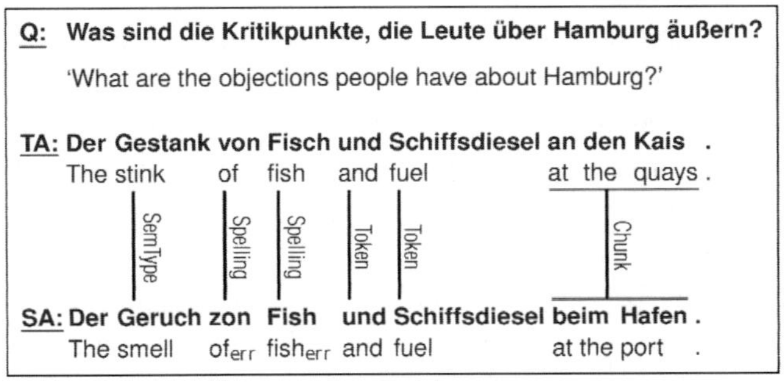

Figure 1: Basic example for alignment approach

As the example suggests, it is not sufficient to align only identical surface forms given that significant lexical and syntactic variation occurs in typical student answers. Alignment thus is supported at different levels of abstraction. For example, the token units are enriched with lemma and synonym information using standard NLP tools. Table 2 gives an overview of which NLP tools we use for which task in CoMiC-DE. In general, the components are very similar to those used in the English system, with different statistical models and parameters where necessary.

Annotation Task	NLP Component
Sentence Detection	OpenNLP http://incubator.apache.org/opennlp
Tokenization	OpenNLP
Lemmatization	TreeTagger (Schmid, 1994)
Spell Checking	Edit distance (Levenshtein, 1966), igerman98 word list http://www.j3e.de/ispell/igerman98
Part-of-speech Tagging	TreeTagger (Schmid, 1994)
Noun Phrase Chunking	OpenNLP
Lexical Relations	GermaNet (Hamp and Feldweg, 1997)
Similarity Scores	PMI-IR (Turney, 2001)
Dependency Relations	MaltParser (Nivre et al., 2007)

Table 2: NLP tools used in the German system

Integrating the multitude of units and their representations at different levels of abstraction poses significant challenges to the system architecture. Among other requirements, different representations of the same surface string need to be stored without interfering with each other, and various NLP tools need to collaborate in order to produce the final rich data structures used for answer comparison. To meet these requirements, we chose to implement our system in the Unstructured Information Management Architecture (UIMA, cf. Ferrucci and Lally, 2004). UIMA allows automatic analysis modules to access layers of stand-off annotation, and hence allows for the coexistence of both independent and interdependent annotations, unlike traditional pipeline-style architectures, where the output of each component replaces its input. The use of UIMA in recent successful large-scale projects such as DeepQA (Ferrucci et al., 2010) confirms that UIMA is a good candidate for complex language processing tasks where integration of various representations is required.

In order to determine the global alignment configuration, all local alignment options are computed for every mappable unit. These local candidates are then used as input for the Traditional Marriage Algorithm (Gale and Shapley, 1962) which computes a global alignment solution where each mappable unit is aligned to at most one unit in the other response, such as the one we saw in Figure 1.

On the basis of the resulting global alignment configuration, the system performs the binary content assessment by evaluating whether the meaning of the learner and the target answer are sufficiently similar. For this purpose, it extracts features which encode the numbers and types of alignment and feeds them to the memory-based classifier TiMBL (Daelemans et al., 2007). The features used are listed in Table 3.

Features	Description
1. Keyword Overlap	Percent of keywords aligned (relative to target)
2./3. Token Overlap	Percent of aligned target/learner tokens
4./5. Chunk Overlap	Percent of aligned target/learner chunks
6./7. Triple Overlap	Percent of aligned target/learner triples
8. Token Match	Percent of token alignments that were token-identical
9. Similarity Match	Percent of token alignments that were similarity-resolved
10. Type Match	Percent of token alignments that were type-resolved
11. Lemma Match	Percent of token alignments that were lemma-resolved
12. Synonym Match	Percent of token alignments that were synonym-resolved
13. Variety of Match (0-5)	Number of kinds of token-level alignments

Table 3: Features used for the memory-based classifier

4 Content Assessment Experiment

4.1 Setup

We ran our content assessment experiment using the two data sets introduced in section 2, one from Kansas University and the other from The Ohio State University. Both of these contain only records where both annotators agreed on the binary assessment (appropriate/inappropriate meaning). Each set is balanced, i.e., they contain the same number of appropriate and inappropriate student answers.

In training and testing the TiMBL-based classifier, we followed the methodology of Bailey (2008, p. 240), where seven classifiers are trained using the different available distance metrics (Overlap, Levenshtein, Numeric Overlap, Modified value difference, Jeffrey divergence, Dot product, Cosine). Training and testing was performed using the *leave-one-out* scheme (Weiss and Kulikowski, 1991) and for each item the output of the seven classifiers was combined via majority voting.

4.2 Results

The classification accuracy for both data sets is summarized in Table 4. We report accuracy and the total number of answers for each data set.

	KU data set	OSU data set
# of answers	610	422
Accuracy	**84.6%**	**84.6%**

Table 4: Classification accuracy for the two data sets

The 84.6% accuracy figure obtained for both data sets shows that CoMiC-DE is quite successful in performing content assessment for the German data collected so far, a result which is competitive with the one for English obtained by Bailey and Meurers (2008), who report an accuracy of 78% for the binary assessment task on a balanced English data set.

A remarkable feature is the identity of the scores for the two data sets, considering that the data was collected at different universities from different students in different classes run by different teachers. Moreover, there was no overlap in exercise material between the two data sets. This indicates that there is some characteristic uniformity of the learner responses in authentic reading comprehension tasks, suggesting that the course setting and task type effectively constrains the degree of syntactic and lexical variation in the student answers. This includes the stage of the learners in this foreign language teaching setting, which limits their exposure to linguistic constructions, as well as the presence of explicit reading texts that the questions are about, which may lead learners to use the lexical material provided instead of rephrasing content in other words. We intend to explore these issues in our future work to obtain a more explicit picture of the contextual and task properties involved.

Another aspect which should be kept in mind is that the scores we obtained are based on a data set for which the two human annotators had agreed on their assessment. We expect automatic classification results to degrade given more controversial data about which human annotators disagree, especially since such data will presumably contain more ambiguous cues, giving rise to multiple interpretations.

4.3 Evaluation by question type

The overall results include many different question types which pose different kinds of challenges to our system. To develop an understanding of those challenges, we performed a more fine-grained evaluation by question types. To distinguish relevant subcases, we applied the question classification scheme introduced by Day and Park (2005). This scheme is more suitable here than other common answer-typing schemata such as the one in Li and Roth (2002), which tend to focus on questions asking for factual knowledge.

Day and Park (2005) distinguish five different question forms: yes/no (question to be answered with either yes or no), alternative (two or more yes/no questions connected with or), true or false (a statement to be classified as true or false), *who/what/when/where/how/why* (*wh*-question containing the respective question word), and multiple choice (choice between several answers presented with a question, of any other question type). In addition, they introduce a second dimension distinguishing the types of comprehension involved, i.e., how the information asked for by the question can be obtained from the text: literal (questions that can be answered directly and explicitly from the text), reorganization (questions where information from various parts of the text must be combined), inference (questions where literal information and world knowledge must be combined), prediction (prediction of how a story might continue), evaluation (comprehensive judgement about aspects of the text) and personal response (personal opinion or feelings about the text or the subject).

Out of the five different forms of question, our data contains questions of all forms except for the multiple choice category and the true or false category given that we are explicitly targeting free text responses. To obtain a more detailed picture of the *wh*-question category, we decided to split that category into its respective *wh*-words and added one more category to it, for *which*. Also, we added the type "several" for questions which contain more than one question presented to the student at a time. Of the six comprehension types, our data contained literal, reorganization and inference questions.

Table 5 reports the accuracy results by question forms and comprehension types for the combined OSU and KU data set. The counts encode the number of student answers for which accuracy is reported (micro-averages). The numbers in brackets specify the number of distinct questions and the corresponding accuracy measures are computed by grouping answers by their question (macro-averages). Comparing answer-based (micro-average) accuracy with question-based (macro-average) accuracy allows us to see whether the results for questions with a high number of answers outweigh questions with a small number of answers. In general the micro- and macro-averages reported are very similar and the overall accuracy is the same (84.6%). Overall, the results thus do not seem to be biased towards a specific, frequently answered question instance. Where larger differences between micro- and macro-averages do arise, as for alternative, *when*, and *where* questions, these are cases with few overall instances in the data set, cautioning us against overinterpreting results for such small subsets. The 4.2% gap for the relatively frequent "several" question type underlines the heterogeneous nature of this class, which may warrant more specific subclasses in the future.

Overall, the accuracy of content assessment for *wh*-questions that can be answered with a concrete piece of information from the text are highest, with 92.6% for "which" questions, and results in the upper 80s for five other *wh*-questions. Interestingly, "who" questions fare comparatively badly, pointing to a relatively high variability in the expression of subjects, which would warrant the integration of a dedicated approach to coreference resolution. Such a direct solution is not available for "why" questions, which at 79.3% is the worst *wh*-question type. The high variability of those answers is rooted in the fact that they ask for a cause or reason, which can be expressed in a multitude of ways, especially for comprehension types involving inferences or reorganization of the information given in the text.

This drop between comprehension types, from literal (86.0%) to inference (81.5%) and reorganization (78.0%), can also be observed throughout and is expected given that the CoMiC-DE system makes use of surface-based alignments where it can find them. For the system to improve on the non-literal comprehension types, features encoding a richer set of abstractions (e.g., to capture distributional similarity at the chunk level or global linguistic phenomena such as negation) need to be introduced.

Just as in the discussion of the micro- and macro-averages above, the "several" question type again rears its ugly heads in terms of a low overall accuracy (77.7%). This supports the conclusion that it requires a dedicated approach. Based on an analysis of the nature and sequence of the component questions, in future work we plan to determine how such combinations constrain the space of variation in acceptable answers.

Finally, while there are few instances for the "alternative" question type, the fact that it resulted in the lowest accuracy (57.1%) warrants some attention. The analysis indeed revealed a general issue, which is discussed in the next section.

5 From eliminating repeated elements to analyzing information structure

Bailey (2008, sec. 5.3.12) observed that answers frequently repeat words given in the question. In her corpus example (1), the first answer repeats "the moral question raised by the Clinton incident" from the question, whereas the second one reformulates this given material. But both sentences essentially answer the question in the same way.[2]

[2]Independent of the issue discussed here, note the presuppo-

	Comprehension type							
	Literal		Reorganization		Inference		Total	
Question type	Acc.	#	Acc.	#	Acc.	#	Acc.	#
Alternative	0	1 (1)	–	0	66.7 (58.3)	6 (3)	57.1 (43.8)	7 (4)
How	85.7 (83.3)	126 (25)	83.3 (77.8)	12 (3)	100	7 (1)	86.2 (83.3)	145 (29)
What	87.0 (87.6)	247 (40)	74.2 (71.7)	31 (4)	83.3 (83.3)	6 (1)	85.6 (86.1)	284 (45)
When	85.7 (93.3)	7 (3)	–	0	–	0	85.7 (93.3)	7 (3)
Where	88.9 (94.4)	9 (3)	–	0	–	0	88.9 (94.4)	9 (3)
Which	92.3 (90.7)	183 (29)	100.0	14 (5)	83.3 (83.3)	6 (2)	92.6 (91.6)	203 (36)
Who	73.9 (80.2)	23 (9)	94.4 (88.9)	18 (3)	–	0	82.9 (82.4)	41 (12)
Why	80.5 (83.3)	128 (17)	57.1 (57.9)	14 (3)	84.4 (81.1)	32 (4)	79.3 (79.7)	174 (24)
Yes/No	–	0	100.0	5 (1)	–	0	100.0	5 (1)
Several	82.1 (85.6)	95 (13)	68.4 (75.1)	38 (5)	75 (74.3)	24 (2)	77.7 (81.9)	157 (20)
Total	86.0 (86)	819 (140)	78.0 (80.7)	132 (24)	81.5 (76.8)	81 (13)	84.6 (84.6)	1032 (177)

Table 5: Accuracy by question form and comprehension types following Day and Park (2005). Counts denoting number of student answers, in brackets: number of questions and macro-average accuracy computed by grouping by questions.

(1) What was the major moral question raised by the Clinton incident?

a. The moral question raised by the Clinton incident was whether a politician's person life is relevant to their job performance.

b. A basic question for the media is whether a politician's personal life is relevant to his or her performance in the job.

The issue arising from the occurrence of such given material for a content assessment approach based on alignment is that all alignments are counted, yet those for given material do not actually contribute to answering the question, as illustrated by the (non)answer containing only given material "The moral question raised by the Clinton incident was whatever." Bailey (2008) concludes that an answer should not be rewarded (or punished) for repeating material that is given in the question and her implementation thus removes all words from the answers which are given in the question.

While such an approach successfully eliminates any contribution from these given words, it has the unfortunate consequence that any NLP processes requiring well-formed complete sentences (such as, e.g., dependency parsers) perform poorly on sentences from which the given words have been removed. In our reimplementation of the approach, we therefore kept the sentences as such intact and instead made use of the UIMA architecture to add a givenness annotation to those words of the answer which are repeated from the question. Such given tokens and any representations derived from them are ignored when the local alignment possibilities are computed.

While successfully replicating the givenness filter of Bailey (2008) without the negative consequences on other NLP analysis, targeting given words in this way is problematic, which becomes particularly apparent when considering examples for the "alternative" question type. In this question type, exemplified in Figure 2 by an example from the KU data set, the answer has to select one of the options from an explicitly given set of alternatives.

Q: Ist die Wohnung in einem Neubau oder einem Altbau?
'Is the flat in a new building or in an old building?'

TA: Die Wohnung ist in einem Neubau .
The flat is in a new building

SA: Die Wohnung ist in einem Neubau
The flat is in a new building

Figure 2: "Alternative" question with answers consisting entirely of given words, resulting in no alignments.

The question asks whether the apartment is in a new or in an old building, and both alternatives are explicitly given in the question. The student picked the same alternative as the one that was selected in the target answer. Indeed, the two answers are identical, but the givenness filter excludes all material from alignment and hence the content assessment

sition failure arising for this authentic reading comprehension question – as far as we see, there was no "major moral question raised by the Clinton incident".

classification fails to identify the student answer as appropriate. This clearly is incorrect and essentially constitutes an opportunity to rethink the givenness filter.

The givenness filter is based on a characterization of the material we want to ignore, which was motivated by the fact that it is easy to identify the material that is repeated from the question. On the other hand, if we analyze the reading comprehension questions more closely, it becomes possible to connect this issue to research in formal pragmatics which investigates the information structure (cf. Krifka, 2007) imposed on a sentence in a discourse addressing an explicit (or implicit) question under discussion (Roberts, 1996). Instead of removing given elements from an answer, under this perspective we want to identify which part of an answer constitutes the so-called focus answering the question.[3]

The advantage of linking our issue to the more general investigation of information structure in linguistics is readily apparent if we consider the significant complexity involved (cf., e.g., Büring, 2007). The issue of asking what constitutes the focus of a sentence is distinct from asking what new information is included in a sentence. New information can be contained in the topic of a sentence. On the other hand, the focus can also contain given information. In (2a), for example, the focus of the answer is "a green apple", even though apples are explicitly given in the question and only the fact that a green one will be bought is new.

(2) You've looked at the apples long enough now, what do you want to buy?
   a. I want to buy a green apple.

In some situations the focus can even consist entirely of given information. This is one way of interpreting what goes on in the case of the alternative questions discussed at the end of the last section. This question type explicitly mentions all alternatives as part of the question, so that the focus of the answer selecting one of those alternatives will typically consist entirely of given information.

As a next step we plan to build on the notion of focus characterized in (a coherent subset of) the information structure literature by developing an approach which identifies the part of an answer which constitutes the focus so that we can limit the alignment procedure on which content assessment is based to the focus of each answer.

[3]The information structure literature naturally also provides a more sophisticated account of givenness. For example, for Schwarzschild (1999), givenness also occurs between hypernyms and coreferent expressions, which would not be detected by the simple surface-based givenness filter included in the current CoMiC-DE.

6 Related Work

There are few systems targeting the short answer evaluation tasks. Most prominent among them is *C-Rater* (Leacock and Chodorow, 2003), a short answer scoring system for English meant for deployment in Intelligent Tutoring Systems (ITS). The authors highlight the fact that *C-Rater* is not simply a string matching program but instead uses more sophisticated NLP such as shallow parsing and synonym matching. *C-Rater* reportedly achieved an accuracy of 84% in two different studies, which is remarkably similar to the scores we report in this paper although clearly the setting and target language differ from ours.

More recently in the ITS field, Nielsen et al. (2009) developed an approach focusing on recognizing textual entailment in student answers. To that end, a corpus of questions and answers was manually annotated with word-word relations, so-called "facets", which represent individual semantic propositions in a particular answer. By learning how to recognize and classify these facets in student answers, the system is then able to give a more differentiated rating of a student answer than "right" or "wrong". We find that this is a promising move in the fields of answer scoring and textual entailment since it also breaks down the complex entailment problem into a set of sub-problems.

7 Conclusion

We presented CoMiC-DE, the first content assessment system for German. For the data used in evaluation so far, CoMiC-DE performs on a competitive level when compared to previous work on English, with accuracy at 84.6%. In addition to these results, we make our reading comprehension corpus freely available for research purposes in order to encourage more work on content assessment and related areas.

In a more detailed evaluation by question and comprehension type, we gained new insights into how question types influence the content assessment tasks. Specifically, our system had more difficulty classifying answers to "why"-questions than other question forms, which we attribute to the fact that causal relations exhibit more form variation than other types of answer material. Also, the comprehension type "reorganization", which requires the reader to collect and combine information from different places in the text, posed more problems to our system than the "literal" type.

Related to the properties of questions, we showed by example that simply marking given material on a surface level is insufficient and a partitioning into focused and background material is needed instead. This is especially relevant for alternative questions, where the exclusion of all given material renders the alignment process useless. Future work will therefore include focus detection in answers and its use in the alignment process. For example, given a weighting scheme for individual alignments, focused material could be weighted more prominently in alignment in order to reflect its importance in assessing the answer.

Acknowledgements

We would like to thank two anonymous TextInfer reviewers for their helpful comments.

References

Stacey Bailey, 2008. Content Assessment in Intelligent Computer-Aided Language Learning: Meaning Error Diagnosis for English as a Second Language. Ph.D. thesis, The Ohio State University. http://osu.worldcat.org/oclc/243467551.

Stacey Bailey and Detmar Meurers, 2008. Diagnosing Meaning Errors in Short Answers to Reading Comprehension Questions. In *Proceedings of the 3rd Workshop on Innovative Use of NLP for Building Educational Applications (BEA-3) at ACL'08*. Columbus, Ohio, pp. 107–115. http://aclweb.org/anthology/W08-0913.

Daniel Büring, 2007. Intonation, Semantics and Information Structure. In Gillian Ramchand and Charles Reiss (eds.), *The Oxford Handbook of Linguistic Interfaces*, Oxford University Press.

Walter Daelemans, Jakub Zavrel, Ko van der Sloot and Antal van den Bosch, 2007. *TiMBL: Tilburg Memory-Based Learner Reference Guide, ILK Technical Report ILK 07-03. Version 6.0.* Tilburg University.

Ido Dagan, Bill Dolan, Bernardo Magnini and Dan Roth, 2009. Recognizing textual entailment: Rational, evaluation and approaches. *Natural Language Engineering*, 15(4):i–xvii.

Richard R. Day and Jeong-Suk Park, 2005. Developing Reading Comprehension Questions. *Reading in a Foreign Language*, 17(1):60–73.

David Ferrucci, Eric Brown et al., 2010. Building Watson: An Overview of the DeepQA Project. *AI Magazine*, 31(3):59–79.

David Ferrucci and Adam Lally, 2004. UIMA: An Architectural Approach to Unstructured Information Processing in the Corporate Research Environment. *Natural Language Engineering*, 10(3–4):327–348.

David Gale and Lloyd S. Shapley, 1962. College Admissions and the Stability of Marriage. *American Mathematical Monthly*, 69:9–15.

Birgit Hamp and Helmut Feldweg, 1997. GermaNet – a Lexical-Semantic Net for German. In *Proceedings of ACL workshop Automatic Information Extraction and Building of Lexical Semantic Resources for NLP Applications*. Madrid. http://aclweb.org/anthology/W97-0802.

Manfred Krifka, 2007. Basic Notions of Information Structure. In Caroline Fery, Gisbert Fanselow and Manfred Krifka (eds.), *The Notions of Information Structure*, Universitätsverlag Potsdam, Potsdam, volume 6 of *Interdisciplinary Studies on Information Structure (ISIS)*.

Thomas Landauer, Peter Foltz and Darrell Laham, 1998. An Introduction to Latent Semantic Analysis. *Discourse Processes*, 25:259–284.

Claudia Leacock and Martin Chodorow, 2003. C-rater: Automated Scoring of Short-Answer Questions. *Computers and the Humanities*, 37:389–405.

Vladimir I. Levenshtein, 1966. Binary Codes Capable of Correcting Deletions, Insertions, and Reversals. *Soviet Physics Doklady*, 10(8):707–710.

Xin Li and Dan Roth, 2002. Learning Question Classifiers. In *Proceedings of the 19th International*

Conference on Computational Linguistics (COLING 2002). Taipei, Taiwan, pp. 1–7.

Detmar Meurers, Niels Ott and Ramon Ziai, 2010. Compiling a Task-Based Corpus for the Analysis of Learner Language in Context. In *Proceedings of Linguistic Evidence*. Tübingen, pp. 214–217. http://purl.org/dm/papers/meurers-ott-ziai-10.html.

Detmar Meurers, Ramon Ziai, Niels Ott and Stacey Bailey, 2011. Integrating Parallel Analysis Modules to Evaluate the Meaning of Answers to Reading Comprehension Questions. *IJCEELL. Special Issue on Automatic Free-text Evaluation*, 21(4):355–369. http://purl.org/dm/papers/meurers-ziai-ott-bailey-11.html.

Rodney D. Nielsen, Wayne Ward and James H. Martin, 2009. Recognizing entailment in intelligent tutoring systems. *Natural Language Engineering*, 15(4):479–501.

Joakim Nivre, Jens Nilsson, Johan Hall, Atanas Chanev, Gülsen Eryigit, Sandra Kübler, Svetoslav Marinov and Erwin Marsi, 2007. MaltParser: A Language-Independent System for Data-Driven Dependency Parsing. *Natural Language Engineering*, 13(1):1–41.

Craige Roberts, 1996. Information Structure in Discourse: Towards an Integrated Formal Theory of Pragmatics. In Jae-Hak Yoon and Andreas Kathol (eds.), *OSU Working Papers in Linguistics No. 49: Papers in Semantics*, The Ohio State University.

Álvaro Rodrigo, Anselmo Peñas and Felisa Verdejo, 2009. Overview of the Answer Validation Exercise 2008. In Carol Peters, Thomas Deselaers, Nicola Ferro, Julio Gonzalo, Gareth Jones, Mikko Kurimo, Thomas Mandl, Anselmo Peñas and Vivien Petras (eds.), *Evaluating Systems for Multilingual and Multimodal Information Access*, Springer Berlin / Heidelberg, volume 5706 of *Lecture Notes in Computer Science*, pp. 296–313.

Helmut Schmid, 1994. Probabilistic Part-of-Speech Tagging Using Decision Trees. In *Proceedings of the International Conference on New Methods in Language Processing*. Manchester, UK, pp. 44–49.

Roger Schwarzschild, 1999. GIVENness, AvoidF and other Constraints on the Placement of Accent. *Natural Language Semantics*, 7(2):141–177.

Karen Spärck Jones, 2007. Automatic Summarising: The State of the Art. *Information Processing and Management*, 43:1449–1481.

Peter Turney, 2001. Mining the Web for Synonyms: PMI-IR Versus LSA on TOEFL. In *Proceedings of the Twelfth European Conference on Machine Learning (ECML-2001)*. Freiburg, Germany, pp. 491–502.

Sholom M. Weiss and Casimir A. Kulikowski, 1991. *Computer Systems That Learn: Classification and Prediction Methods from Statistics, Neural Nets, Machine Learning, and Expert Systems*. Morgan Kaufmann, San Mateo, CA.

Towards a Probabilistic Model for Lexical Entailment

Eyal Shnarch
Computer Science Department
Bar-Ilan University
Ramat-Gan, Israel
shey@cs.biu.ac.il

Jacob Goldberger
School of Engineering
Bar-Ilan University
Ramat-Gan, Israel
goldbej@eng.biu.ac.il

Ido Dagan
Computer Science Department
Bar-Ilan University
Ramat-Gan, Israel
dagan@cs.biu.ac.il

Abstract

While modeling entailment at the lexical-level is a prominent task, addressed by most textual entailment systems, it has been approached mostly by heuristic methods, neglecting some of its important aspects. We present a probabilistic approach for this task which covers aspects such as differentiating various resources by their reliability levels, considering the length of the entailed sentence, the number of its covered terms and the existence of multiple evidence for the entailment of a term. The impact of our model components is validated by evaluations, which also show that its performance is in line with the best published entailment systems.

1 Introduction

Textual Entailment was proposed as a generic paradigm for applied semantic inference (Dagan et al., 2006). Given two textual fragments, termed *hypothesis* (H) and *text* (T), the text is said to textually entail the hypothesis ($T \rightarrow H$) if a person reading the text can infer the meaning of the hypothesis. Since it was first introduced, the six rounds of the Recognizing Textual Entailment (RTE) challenges[1] have become a standard benchmark for entailment systems.

Entailment systems apply various techniques to tackle this task, including logical inference (Tatu and Moldovan, 2007; MacCartney and Manning, 2007), semantic analysis (Burchardt et al., 2007) and syntactic parsing (Bar-Haim et al., 2008; Wang et al., 2009). Inference at these levels usually requires substantial processing and resources, aiming at high performance. Nevertheless, simple *lexical* level entailment systems pose strong baselines which most complex entailment systems did not outperform (Mirkin et al., 2009a; Majumdar and Bhattacharyya, 2010). Additionally, within a complex system, lexical entailment modeling is one of the most effective component. Finally, the simpler lexical approach can be used in cases where complex systems cannot be used, e.g. when there is no parser for a targeted language.

For these reasons lexical entailment systems are widely used. They derive *sentence-level* entailment decision base on *lexical-level* entailment evidence. Typically, this is done by quantifying the degree of lexical coverage of the hypothesis terms by the text terms (where a term may be multi-word). A hypothesis term is covered by a text term if either they are identical (possibly at the stem or lemma level) or there is a lexical entailment *rule* suggesting the entailment of the former by the latter. Such rules are derived from lexical semantic resources, such as WordNet (Fellbaum, 1998), which capture lexical entailment relations.

Common heuristics for quantifying the degree of coverage are setting a threshold on the percentage of coverage of H's terms (Majumdar and Bhattacharyya, 2010), counting the absolute number of uncovered terms (Clark and Harrison, 2010), or applying an Information Retrieval-style vector space similarity score (MacKinlay and Baldwin, 2009). Other works (Corley and Mihalcea, 2005; Zanzotto and Moschitti, 2006) have applied heuristic formu-

[1] http://www.nist.gov/tac/

las to estimate the similarity between text fragments based on a similarity function between their terms.

The above mentioned methods do not capture several important aspects of entailment. Such aspects include the varying reliability levels of entailment resources and the impact of rule chaining and multiple evidence on entailment likelihood. An additional observation from these and other systems is that their performance improves only moderately when utilizing lexical-semantic resources[2].

We believe that the textual entailment field would benefit from more principled models for various entailment phenomena. In this work we formulate a concrete generative probabilistic modeling framework that captures the basic aspects of lexical entailment. A first step in this direction was proposed in Shnarch et al. (2011) (a short paper), where we presented a base model with a somewhat complicated and difficult to estimate extension to handle coverage. This paper extends that work to a more mature model with new extensions.

We first consider the "logical" structure of lexical entailment reasoning and then interpret it in probabilistic terms. Over this base model we suggest several extensions whose significance is then assessed by our evaluations. Learning the parameters of a lexical model poses a challenge since there are no lexical-level entailment annotations. We do, however, have sentence-level annotations available for the RTE data sets. To bridge this gap, we formulate an instance of the EM algorithm (Dempster et al., 1977) to estimate hidden lexical-level entailment parameters from sentence-level annotations.

Overall, we suggest that the main contribution of this paper is in presenting a probabilistic model for lexical entailment. Such a model can better integrate entailment indicators and has the advantage of being able to utilize well-founded probabilistic methods such as the EM algorithm. Our model's performance is in line with the best entailment systems, while opening up directions for future improvements.

2 Background

We next review several entailment systems, mostly those that work at the lexical level and in particular those with which we compare our results on the RTE data sets.

The 5th Recognizing Textual Entailment challenge (RTE-5) introduced a new pilot task (Bentivogli et al., 2009) which became the main task in RTE-6 (Bentivogli et al., 2010). In this task the goal is to find all sentences that entail each hypothesis in a given document cluster. This task's data sets reflect a natural distribution of entailments in a corpus and demonstrate a more realistic scenario than the earlier RTE challenges.

As reviewed in the following paragraphs there are several characteristic in common to most entailment systems: (1) lexical resources have a minimal impact on their performance, (2) they heuristically utilize lexical resources, and (3) there is no principled method for making the final entailment decision.

The best performing system of RTE-5 was presented by Mirkin et. al (2009a). It applies supervised classifiers over a parse tree representations to identify entailment. They reported that utilizing lexical resources only slightly improved their performance.

MacKinlay and Baldwin (2009) presented the best lexical-level system at RTE-5. They use a vector space method to measure the lexical overlap between the text and the hypothesis. Since usually texts of RTE are longer than their corresponding hypotheses, the standard cosine similarity score came out lower than expected. To overcome this problem they suggested a simple ad-hoc variant of the cosine similarity score which removed from the text all terms which did not appear in the corresponding hypothesis. While this heuristic improved performance considerably, they reported a decrease in performance when utilizing synonym and derivation relations from WordNet.

On the RTE-6 data set, the syntactic-based system of Jia et. al (2010) achieved the best results, only slightly higher than the lexical-level system of (Majumdar and Bhattacharyya, 2010). The latter utilized several resources for matching hypothesis terms with text terms: WordNet, VerbOcean (Chklovski and Pantel, 2004), utilizing two of its relations, as well as an acronym database, number matching module, co-reference resolution and named entity recognition tools. Their final entailment decision was based on a threshold over the

[2]See ablation tests reports in http://aclweb.org/aclwiki/ index.php?title=RTE_Knowledge_Resources#Ablation_Tests

number of matched hypothesis terms. They found out that hypotheses of different length require different thresholds.

While the above systems measure the number of hypothesis terms matched by the text, Clark and Harrison (2010) based their entailment decision on the number of *mismatched* hypothesis terms. They utilized both WordNet and the DIRT paraphrase database (Lin and Pantel, 2001). With WordNet, they used one set of relations to identify the concept of a term while another set of relations was used to identify entailment between concepts. Their results were inconclusive about the overall effect of DIRT while WordNet produced a net benefit in most configurations. They have noticed that setting a global threshold for the entailment decision, decreased performance for some topics of the RTE-6 data set. Therefore, they tuned a varying threshold for each topic based on an idiosyncracy of the data, by which the total number of entailments per topic is approximately a constant.

Glickman et al. (2005) presented a simple model that recasted the lexical entailment task as a variant of text classification and estimated entailment probabilities solely from co-occurrence statistics. Their model did not utilize any lexical resources.

In contrary to these systems, our model shows improvement when utilizing high quality resources such as WordNet and the CatVar (Categorial Variation) database (Habash and Dorr, 2003). As Majumdar and Bhattacharyya (2010), our model considers the impact of hypothesis length, however it does not require the tuning of a unique threshold for each length. Finally, most of the above systems do not differentiate between the various lexical resources they use, even though it is known that resources reliability vary considerably (Mirkin et al., 2009b). Our probabilistic model, on the other hand, learns a unique reliability parameter for each resource it utilizes. As mentioned above, this work extends the base model in (Shnarch et al., 2011), which is described in the next section.

3 A Probabilistic Model

We aim at obtaining a probabilistic score for the likelihood that the hypothesis terms are entailed by the terms of the text. There are several prominent aspects of entailment, mostly neglected by previous lexical methods, which our model aims to capture: (1) the reliability variability of different lexical resources; (2) the effect of the length of transitive rule application chain on the likelihood of its validity; and (3) addressing cases of multiple entailment evidence when entailing a term.

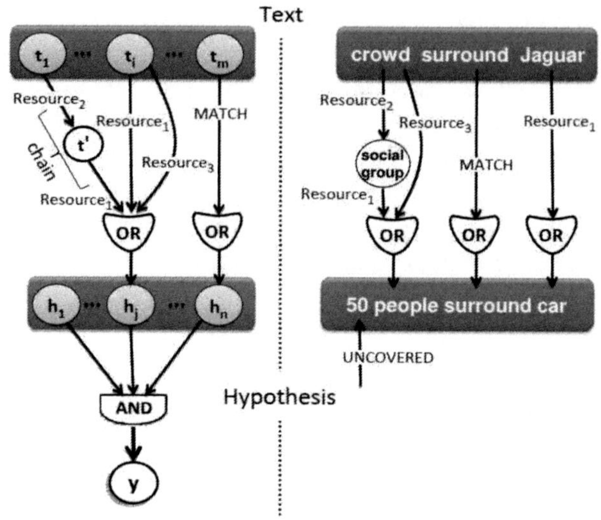

Figure 1: **Left:** the base model of entailing a hypothesis from a text; **Right:** a concrete example for it (stop-words removed). Edges in the upper part of the diagram represent entailment rules. Rules compose chains through AND gates (omitted for visual clarity). Chains are gathered by OR gates to entail terms, and the final entailment decision y is the result of their AND gate.

3.1 The Base Model

Our base model follows the one presented in (Shnarch et al., 2011), which is described here in detail to make the current paper self contained.

3.1.1 Entailment generation process

We first specify the process by which a decision of lexical entailment between T and H using knowledge resources should be determined, as illustrated in Figure 1 (a general description on the left and a concrete example on the right). There are two ways by which a term $h \in H$ is entailed by a term $t \in T$. A direct MATCH is the case in which t and h are identical terms (possibly at the stem or lemma level). Alternatively, lexical entailment can be established based on knowledge of entailing lexical-semantic relations, such as synonyms, hypernyms and morphological derivations, available in lexical resources. These relations provide *lexical entailment rules*, e.g. *Jaguar* $\rightarrow$ *car*. We denote the resource which provided the rule r by $R(r)$.

It should be noticed at this point that such rules specify a lexical entailment relation that might hold for *some* (T, H) pairs but not necessarily for all pairs, e.g. the rule *Jaguar* $\rightarrow$ *car* does not hold in the wildlife context. Thus, the application of an available rule to infer lexical entailment in a given (T, H) pair might be either valid or invalid. We note here the difference between *covering* a term and *entailing* it. A term is covered when the available resources suggest its entailment. However, since a rule application may be invalid for the particular (T, H) context, a term is entailed only if there is a valid rule application from T to it.

Entailment is a transitive relation, therefore rules may compose transitive *chains* that connect t to h via intermediate term(s) t' (e.g. *crowd* $\rightarrow$ *social group* $\rightarrow$ *people*). For a chain to be valid for the current (T, H) pair, *all* its composing rule applications should be valid for this pair. This corresponds to a logical AND gate (omitted in Figure 1 for visual clarity) which takes as input the validity values (1/0) of the individual rule applications.

Next, multiple chains may connect t to h (as for t_i and h_j in Figure 1) or connect several terms in T to h (as t_1 and t_i are indicating the entailment of h_j in Figure 1), thus providing multiple evidence for h's entailment. For a term h to be entailed by T it is enough that *at least one* of the chains from T to h would be valid. This condition is realized in the model by an OR gate. Finally, for T to *lexically* entail H it is usually assumed that *every* $h \in H$ should be entailed by T (Glickman et al., 2006). Therefore, the final decision follows an AND gate combining the entailment decisions for all hypothesis terms. Thus, the 1-bit outcome of this gate y corresponds to the sentence-level entailment status.

3.1.2 Probabilistic Setting

When assessing entailment for (T, H) pair, we do not know for sure which rule applications are valid. Taking a probabilistic perspective, we assume a parameter θ_R for each resource R, denoting its reliability, i.e. the prior probability that applying a rule from R for an arbitrary (T, H) pair corresponds to valid entailment[3]. Under this perspective, direct MATCHs are considered as rules coming from a special "resource", for which θ_{MATCH} is expected to be close to 1. Additionally, there could be a term h which is not covered by any of the resources at hand, whose coverage is inevitably incomplete. We assume that each such h is covered by a single rule coming from a dummy resource called UNCOVERED, while expecting $\theta_{\text{UNCOVERED}}$ to be relatively small. Based on the θ_R values we can now estimate, for each entailment inference step in Figure 1, the probability that this step is valid (the corresponding bit is 1).

Equations (1) - (3) correspond to the three steps in calculating the probability for entailing a hypothesis.

$$p(t \xrightarrow{c} h) = \prod_{r \in c} p(L \xrightarrow{r} R) = \prod_{r \in c} \theta_{R(r)} \quad (1)$$

$$p(T \rightarrow h) = 1 - p(T \nrightarrow h) = 1 - \prod_{c \in C(h)} [1 - p(t \xrightarrow{c} h)] \quad (2)$$

$$p(T \rightarrow H) = \prod_{h \in H} p(T \rightarrow h) \quad (3)$$

First, Eq. (1) specifies the probability of a particular chain c, connecting a text term t to a hypothesis term h, to correspond to a valid entailment between t and h. This event is denoted by $t \xrightarrow{c} h$ and its probability is the joint probability that the applications of all rules $r \in c$ are valid. Note that every rule r in a chain c connects two terms, its left-hand-side L and its right-hand-side R. The left-hand-side of the first rule in c is $t \in T$ and the right-hand-side of the last rule in it is $h \in H$. Let us denote the event of a valid rule application by $L \xrightarrow{r} R$. Since a-priori a rule r is valid with probability $\theta_{R(r)}$, and assuming independence of all $r \in c$, we obtain Eq. (1).

Next, Eq. (2) utilizes Eq. (1) to specify the probability that T entails h (at least by one chain). Let $C(h)$ denote the set of chains which suggest the entailment of h. The requested probability is equal to 1 minus the probability of the complement event, that is, T does not entail h by any chain. The latter probability is the product of probabilities that all

[3]Modeling a conditional probability for the validity of r, which considers contextual aspects of r's validity in the current (T, H) context, is beyond the scope of this paper (see discussion in Section 6)

chains $c \in C(h)$ are not valid (again assuming independence of chains).

Finally, Eq. (3) gives the probability that T entails all of H ($T \rightarrow H$), assuming independence of H's terms. This is the probability that every $h \in H$ is entailed by T, as specified by Eq. (2).

Altogether, these formulas fall out of the standard probabilistic estimate for the output of AND and OR gates when assuming independence amongst their input bits.

As can be seen, the base model distinguishes varying resource reliabilities, as captured by θ_R, decreases entailment probability as rule chain grows, having more elements in the product of Eq. (1), and increases it when entailment of a term is supported by multiple chains with more inputs to the OR gate. Next we describe two extensions for this base model which address additional important phenomena of lexical entailment.

3.2 Relaxing the AND Gate

Based on term-level decisions for the entailment of each $h \in H$, the model has to produce a sentence-level decision of $T \rightarrow H$. In the model described so far, for T to entail H it must entail *all* its terms. This demand is realized by the AND gate at the bottom of Figure 1. In practice, this demand is too strict, and we would like to leave some option for entailing H even if not every $h \in H$ is entailed. Thus, it is desired to relax this strict demand enforced by the AND gate in the model.

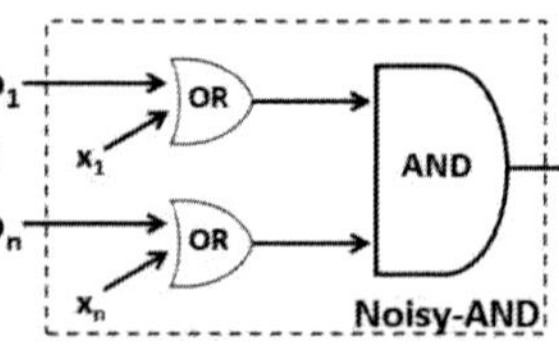

Figure 2: A noisy-AND gate

The Noisy-AND model (Pearl, 1988), depicted in Figure 2, is a soft probabilistic version of the AND gate, which is often used to describe the interaction between causes and their common effect. In this variation, each one of the binary inputs $b_1, ..., b_n$ of the AND gate is first joined with a "noise" bit x_i by an OR gate. Each "noise" bit is 1 with probability p, which is the parameter of the gate. The output bit y is defined as:

$$y = (b_1 \vee x_1) \wedge (b_2 \vee x_2) \wedge \cdots \wedge (b_n \vee x_n)$$

and the conditional probability for it to be 1 is:

$$p(y = 1 | b_1, ..., b_n, n) = \prod_{i=1}^{n} p^{(1-b_i)} = p^{(n - \sum_i b_i)}$$

If all the binary input values are 1, the output is deterministically 1. Otherwise, the probability that the output is 1 is proportional to the number of ones in the input, where the distribution depends on the parameter p. In case $p = 0$ the model reduces to the regular AND.

In our model we replace the final strict AND with a noisy-AND, thus increasing the probability of T to entail H, to account for the fact that sometimes H might be entailed from T even though some $h \in H$ is not directly entailed.

The input size n for the noisy-AND is the length of the hypotheses and therefore it varies from H to H. Had we used the same model parameter p for all lengths, the probability to output 1 would have depended solely on the number of 0 bits in the input without considering the number of ones. For example, the probability to entail a hypothesis with 10 terms given that 8 of them are entailed by T (and 2 are not) is p^2. The same probability is obtained for a hypothesis of length 3 with a single entailed term. We, however, expect the former to have a higher probability since a larger portion of its terms is entailed by T.

There are many ways to incorporate the length of a hypothesis into the noisy-AND model in order to normalize its parameter. The approach we take is defining a separate parameter p_n for each hypothesis length n such that $p_n = \theta_{NA}^{\frac{1}{n}}$, where θ_{NA} becomes the underlying parameter value of the noisy-AND, i.e.

$$p(y = 1 | b_1, ..., b_n, n) = p_n^{(n - \sum b_i)} = \theta_{NA}^{\frac{n - \sum b_i}{n}}$$

This way, if non of the hypothesis terms is entailed, the probability for its entailment is θ_{NA}, independent of its length:

$$p(y = 1 | 0, 0, ..., 0, n) = p_n^n = \theta_{NA}$$

As can be seen from Figure 1, replacing the final AND gate by a noisy-AND gate is equivalent to adding an additional chain to the OR gate of each hypothesis term. Therefore we update Eq. (2) to:

$$\begin{aligned} p(T \rightarrow h) =& 1 - p(T \nrightarrow h) \\ =& 1 - [(1 - \theta_{NA}^{\frac{1}{n}}) \cdot \prod_{c \in C(h)} [1 - p(t \xrightarrow{c} h)]] \end{aligned} \quad (2^*)$$

In the length-normalized noisy-AND model the value of the parameter p becomes higher for longer hypotheses. This increases the probability to entail such hypotheses, compensating for the lower probability to strictly entail all of their terms.

3.3 Considering Coverage Level

The second extension of the base model follows our observation that the prior validity likelihood for a rule application, increases as more of H's terms are covered by the available resources. In other words, if we have a hypothesis H_1 with k covered terms and a hypothesis H_2 in which only $j < k$ terms are covered, then an arbitrary rule application for H_1 is more likely to be valid than an arbitrary rule application for H_2.

We chose to model this phenomenon by normalizing the reliability θ_R of each resource according to the number of covered terms in H. The normalization is done in a similar manner to the length-normalized noisy-AND described above, obtaining a modified version of Eq. (1):

$$p(t \xrightarrow{c} h) = \prod_{r \in c} \theta_{R(r)}^{\frac{1}{\#covered}} \quad (1^*)$$

As a results, the larger the number of covered terms is, the larger θ_R values our model uses and, in total, the entailment probability increases.

To sum up, we have presented the base model, providing a probabilistic estimate for the entailment status in our generation process specified in 3.1. Two extensions were then suggested: one that relaxes the strict AND gate and normalizes this relaxation by the length of the hypothesis; the second extension adjusts the validity of rule applications as a function of the number of the hypothesis covered terms. Overall, our *full model* combines both extensions over the base probabilistic model.

4 Parameter Estimation

The difficulty in estimating the θ_R values from training data arises because these are term-level parameters while the RTE-training entailment annotation is given for the sentence-level, each (T, H) pair in the training is annotated as either entailing or not. Therefore, we use an instance of the EM algorithm (Dempster et al., 1977) to estimate these hidden parameters.

4.1 E-Step

In the E-step, for each application of a rule r in a chain c for $h \in H$ in a training pair (T, H), we compute $w_{hcr}(T, H)$, the posterior probability that the rule application was valid given the training annotation:

$$w_{hcr}(T, H) = \begin{cases} p(L \xrightarrow{r} R | T \rightarrow H) & \text{if } T \rightarrow H \\ p(L \xrightarrow{r} R | T \nrightarrow H) & \text{if } T \nrightarrow H \end{cases} \quad (4)$$

where the two cases refer to whether the training pair is annotated as entailing or non-entailing. For simplicity, we write w_{hcr} when the (T, H) context is clear.

The E-step can be efficiently computed using dynamic programming as follows; For each training pair (T, H) we first compute the probability $p(T \rightarrow H)$ and keep all the intermediate computations (Eq. (1)- (3)). Then, the two cases of Eq. (4), elaborated next, can be computed from these expressions. For computing Eq. (4) in the case that $T \rightarrow H$ we have:

$$p(L \xrightarrow{r} R | T \rightarrow H) = p(L \xrightarrow{r} R | T \rightarrow h) = \frac{p(T \rightarrow h | L \xrightarrow{r} R) p(L \xrightarrow{r} R)}{p(T \rightarrow h)}$$

The first equality holds since when T entails H every $h \in H$ is entailed by it. Then we apply Bayes' rule. We have already computed the denominator (Eq. (2)), $p(L \xrightarrow{r} R) \equiv \theta_{R(r)}$ and it can be shown[4] that:

$$p(T \rightarrow h | L \xrightarrow{r} R) = 1 - \frac{p(T \nrightarrow h)}{1 - p(t \xrightarrow{c} h)} \cdot (1 - \frac{p(t \xrightarrow{c} h)}{\theta_{R(r)}}) \quad (5)$$

[4]The first and second denominators reduce elements from the products in Eq. 2 and Eq. 1 correspondingly

where c is the chain which contains the rule r.

For computing Eq. (4), in the second case, that $T \nrightarrow H$, we have:

$$p(L \xrightarrow{r} R | T \nrightarrow H) = \frac{p(T \nrightarrow H | L \xrightarrow{r} R) p(L \xrightarrow{r} R)}{p(T \nrightarrow H)}$$

In analogy to Eq. (5) it can be shown that

$$p(T \nrightarrow H | L \xrightarrow{r} R) = 1 - \frac{p(T \rightarrow H)}{p(T \rightarrow h)} \cdot p(T \rightarrow h | L \xrightarrow{r} R) \quad (6)$$

while the expression for $p(T \rightarrow h | L \xrightarrow{r} R)$ appears in Eq. (5).

This efficient computation scheme is an instance of the belief-propagation algorithm (Pearl, 1988) applied to the entailment process, which is a loop-free directed graph (Bayesian network).

4.2 M-Step

In the M-step we need to maximize the EM auxiliary function $Q(\theta)$ where θ is the set of all resources reliability values. Applying the derivation of the auxiliary function to our model (first without the extensions) we obtain:

$$Q(\theta) = \sum_{T,H} \sum_{h \in H} \sum_{c \in C(h)} \sum_{r \in c} (w_{hcr} \log \theta_{R(r)} + (1 - w_{hcr}) \log(1 - \theta_{R(r)}))$$

We next denote by n_R the total number of applications of rules from resource R in the training data. We can maximize $Q(\theta)$ for each R separately to obtain the M-step parameter-updating formula:

$$\theta_R = \frac{1}{n_R} \sum_{T,H} \sum_{h \in H} \sum_{c \in C(h)} \sum_{r \in c | R(r) = R} w_{hcr} \quad (7)$$

The updated parameter value averages the posterior probability that rules from resource R have been validly applied, across all its utilizations in the training data.

4.3 EM for the Extended Model

In case we normalize the noisy-AND parameter by the hypothesis length, for each length we use a different parameter value for the noisy-AND and we cannot simply merge the information from all the training pairs (T, H). To find the optimal parameter value for θ_{NA}, we need to maximize the following expression (the derivation of the auxiliary function to the hypothesis-length-normalized noisy-AND "resource"):

$$Q(\theta_{NA}) = \sum_{T,H} \sum_{h \in H} (w_{hNA} \log(\theta_{NA}^{\frac{1}{n}}) + (1 - w_{hNA}) \log(1 - \theta_{NA}^{\frac{1}{n}})) \quad (8)$$

where n is the length of H, θ_{NA} is the parameter value of the noisy-AND model and w_{hNA} is the posterior probability that the noisy-AND was used to validly entail the term h[5], i.e.

$$w_{hNA}(T, H) = \begin{cases} p(T \xrightarrow{NA} h | T \rightarrow H) & \text{if } T \rightarrow H \\ p(T \xrightarrow{NA} h | T \nrightarrow H) & \text{if } T \nrightarrow H \end{cases}$$

The two cases of the above equation are similar to Eq. (4) and can be efficiently computed in analogy to Eq. (5) and Eq. (6).

There is no close-form expression for the parameter value θ_{NA} that maximizes expression (8). Since $\theta_{NA} \in [0, 1]$ is a scalar parameter, we can find θ_{NA} value that maximizes $Q(\theta_{NA})$ using an exhaustive grid search on the interval $[0, 1]$, in each iteration of the M-step. Alternatively, for an iterative procedure to maximize expression (8), see Appendix A.

In the same manner we address the normalization of the reliability θ_R of each resources R by the number of H's covered terms. Expression (8) becomes:

$$Q(\theta_R) = \sum_{T,H} \sum_{h \in H} \sum_{c \in C(h)} \sum_{r \in c | R(r) = R} (w_{hcr} \log(\theta_R^{cov}) + (1 - w_{hcr}) \log(1 - \theta_R^{cov}))$$

were $\frac{1}{cov}$ is the number of H terms which are covered. We can find the θ_R that maximizes this equation in one of the methods described above.

5 Evaluation and Results

For our evaluation we use the RTE-5 pilot task and the RTE-6 main task data sets described in Section 2. In our system, sentences are tokenized and stripped of stop words and terms are tagged for part-of-speech and lemmatized. We utilized two lexical resources, WordNet (Fellbaum, 1998) and CatVar

[5] In contrary to Eq. 4, here there is no specific $t \in T$ that entails h, therefore we write $T \xrightarrow{NA} h$

(Habash and Dorr, 2003). From WordNet we took as entailment rules synonyms, derivations, hyponyms and meronyms of the first senses of T and H terms. CatVar is a database of clusters of uninflected words (lexemes) and their categorial (i.e. part-of-speech) variants (e.g. announce (verb), announcer and announcement(noun) and announced (adjective)). We deduce an entailment relation between any two lexemes in the same cluster. Model's parameters were estimated from the development set, taken as training. Based on these parameters, the entailment probability was estimated for each pair (T, H) in the test set, and the classification threshold was tuned by classification over the development set.

We next present our evaluation results. First we investigate the impact of utilizing lexical resources and of chaining rules. In section 5.2 we evaluate the contribution of each extension of the base model and in Section 5.3 we compare our performance to that of state-of-the-art entailment systems.

5.1 Resources and Rule-Chaining Impact

As mentioned in Section 2, in the RTE data sets it is hard to show more than a moderate improvement when utilizing lexical resources. Our analysis ascribes this fact to the relatively small amount of rule applications in both data sets. For instance, in RTE-6 there are 10 times more direct matches of identical terms than WordNet and CatVar rule applications combined, while in RTE-5 this ratio is 6. As a result the impact of rule applications can be easily shadowed by the large amount of direct matches.

Table 1 presents the performance of our (full) model when utilizing *no resources* at all, *WordNet*, *CatVar* and both, with chains of a single step. We also considered rule chains of length up to 4 and present here the results of 2 chaining steps with *WordNet-2* and *(WordNet+CatVar)-2*.

Overall, despite the low level of rule applications, we see that incorporating lexical resources in our model significantly[6] and quite consistently improves performance over using no resources at all. Naturally, the optimal combination of resources may vary somewhat across the data sets.

In RTE-6 *WordNet-2* significantly improved performance over the single-stepped WordNet. However, mostly chaining did not help, suggesting the need for future work to improve chain modeling in our framework.

Model	$F_1\%$ RTE-5	$F_1\%$ RTE-6
no resources	41.6	44.9
WordNet	45.8	44.6
WordNet-2	45.7	45.5
CatVar	46.9	**45.6**
WordNet + CatVar	**48.3**	**45.6**
(WordNet + CatVar)-2	47.1	44.0

Table 1: Evaluation of the impact of resources and chaining.

5.2 Model Components impact

We next assess the impact of each of our proposed extensions to the base probabilistic model. To that end, we incorporate *WordNet+CatVar* (our best configuration above) as resources for the *base model* (Section 3.1) and compare it with the *noisy-AND* extension (Eq. (2*)), the *covered-norm* extension which normalizes the resource reliability parameter by the number of covered terms (Eq. (1*)) and the *full model* which combines both extensions. Table 2 presents the results: both *noisy-AND* and *covered-norm* extensions significantly increase F_1 over the base model (by 4.5-8.4 points). This scale of improvement was observed with all resources and chain-length combinations. In both data sets, the combination of *noisy-AND* and *covered-norm* extensions in the full model significantly outperforms each of them separately[7], showing their complementary nature. We also observed that applying noisy-AND without the hypothesis length normalization hardly improved performance over the base model, emphasising the importance of considering hypothesis length. Overall, we can see that both base model extensions improve performance.

Table 3 illustrates a set of maximum likelihood parameters that yielded our best results (*full model*). The parameter value indicates the learnt reliability of the corresponding resource.

[6] All significant results in this section are according to McNemar's test with $p < 0.01$ unless stated otherwise

[7] With the following exception: in RTE-5 the full model is better than the *noisy-AND* extension with significance of only $p = 0.06$

Model	F_1%	
	RTE-5	RTE-6
base model	36.2	38.5
noisy-AND	44.6	43.1
covered-norm	42.8	44.7
full model	**48.3**	**45.6**

Table 2: Impact of model components.

θ_{MATCH}	θ_{WORDNET}	θ_{CATVAR}	$\theta_{\text{UNCOVERED}}$	θ_{NA}
0.80	0.70	0.65	0.17	0.05

Table 3: A parameter set of the *full model* which maximizes the likelihood of the training set.

5.3 Comparison to Prior Art

Finally, in Table 4, we put these results in the context of the best published results on the RTE task. We compare our model to the *average* of the best runs of all systems, the *best* and *second best* performing lexical systems and the *best full system* of each challenge. For both data sets our model is situated high above the average system. For the RTE-6 data set, our model's performance is third best with Majumdar and Bhattacharyya (2010) being the only lexical-level system which outperforms it. However, their system utilized additional processing that we did not, such as named entity recognition and co-reference resolution[8]. On the RTE-5 data set our model outperforms any other published result.

Model	F_1%	
	RTE-5	RTE-6
full model	48.3	45.6
avg. of all systems	30.5	33.8
2nd best lexical system	40.3^a	44.0^b
best lexical system	44.4^c	47.6^d
best full system	45.6^c	48.0^e

Table 4: Comparison to RTE-5 and RTE-6 best entailment systems: (a)(MacKinlay and Baldwin, 2009), (b)(Clark and Harrison, 2010), (c)(Mirkin et al., 2009a)(2 submitted runs), (d)(Majumdar and Bhattacharyya, 2010) and (e)(Jia et al., 2010).

[8]We note that the submitted run which outperformed our result utilized a threshold which was a manual modification of the threshold obtained systematically in another run. The latter run achieved F_1 of 42.4% which is below our result.

We conclude that our probabilistic model demonstrates quality results which are also consistent, without applying heuristic methods of the kinds reviewed in Section 2

6 Conclusions and Future Work

We presented, a probabilistic model for lexical entailment whose innovations are in (1) considering each lexical resource separately by associating an individual reliability value for it, (2) considering the existence of multiple evidence for term entailment and its impact on entailment assessment, (3) setting forth a probabilistic method to relax the strict demand that all hypothesis terms must be entailed, and (4) taking account of the number of covered terms in modeling entailment reliability.

We addressed the impact of the various components of our model and showed that its performance is in line with the best state-of-the-art inference systems. Future work is still needed to reflect the impact of transitivity. We consider replacing the AND gate on the rules of a chain by a noisy-AND, to relax its strict demand that all its input rules must be valid. Additionally, we would like to integrate Contextual Preferences (Szpektor et al., 2008) and other works on Selectional Preference (Erk and Pado, 2010) to verify the validity of the application of a rule in a specific (T, H) context. We also intend to explore the contribution of our model within a complex system that integrates multiple levels of inference as well as its contribution for other applications, such as Passage Retrieval.

References

Roy Bar-Haim, Jonathan Berant, Ido Dagan, Iddo Greental, Shachar Mirkin, Eyal Shnarch, and Idan Szpektor. 2008. Efficient semantic deduction and approximate matching over compact parse forests. In *Proc. of TAC*.

Luisa Bentivogli, Ido Dagan, Hoa Trang Dang, Danilo Giampiccolo, and Bernardo Magnini. 2009. The fifth PASCAL recognizing textual entailment challenge. In *Proc. of TAC*.

Luisa Bentivogli, Peter Clark, Ido Dagan, Hoa Trang Dang, and Danilo Giampiccolo. 2010. The sixth PASCAL recognizing textual entailment challenge. In *Proc. of TAC*.

Aljoscha Burchardt, Nils Reiter, Stefan Thater, and Anette Frank. 2007. A semantic approach to textual entailment: System evaluation and task analysis. In *Proc. of the ACL-PASCAL Workshop on Textual Entailment and Paraphrasing*.

Timothy Chklovski and Patrick Pantel. 2004. Verbocean: Mining the web for fine-grained semantic verb relations. In *Proc. of EMNLP*.

Peter Clark and Phil Harrison. 2010. BLUE-Lite: a knowledge-based lexical entailment system for RTE6. In *Proc. of TAC*.

Courtney Corley and Rada Mihalcea. 2005. Measuring the semantic similarity of texts. In *Proc. of the ACL Workshop on Empirical Modeling of Semantic Equivalence and Entailment*.

Ido Dagan, Oren Glickman, and Bernardo Magnini. 2006. The PASCAL recognising textual entailment challenge. In *Lecture Notes in Computer Science*, volume 3944, pages 177–190.

A. P. Dempster, N. M. Laird, and D. B. Rubin. 1977. Maximum likelihood from incomplete data via the EM algorithm. *Journal of the royal statistical society, series [B]*, 39(1):1–38.

Katrin Erk and Sebastian Pado. 2010. Exemplar-based models for word meaning in context. In *Proc. of the ACL*.

Christiane Fellbaum, editor. 1998. *WordNet: An Electronic Lexical Database (Language, Speech, and Communication)*. The MIT Press.

Oren Glickman, Ido Dagan, and Moshe Koppel. 2005. A probabilistic classification approach for lexical textual entailment. In *Proc. of AAAI*.

Oren Glickman, Eyal Shnarch, and Ido Dagan. 2006. Lexical reference: a semantic matching subtask. In *Proceedings of the EMNLP*.

Nizar Habash and Bonnie Dorr. 2003. A categorial variation database for english. In *Proc. of NAACL*.

Houping Jia, Xiaojiang Huang, Tengfei Ma, Xiaojun Wan, and Jianguo Xiao. 2010. PKUTM participation at TAC 2010 RTE and summarization track. In *Proc. of TAC*.

Dekang Lin and Patrick Pantel. 2001. Discovery of inference rules for question answering. *Natural Language Engineering*, 7:343–360.

Bill MacCartney and Christopher D. Manning. 2007. Natural logic for textual inference. In *Proc. of the ACL-PASCAL Workshop on Textual Entailment and Paraphrasing*.

Andrew MacKinlay and Timothy Baldwin. 2009. A baseline approach to the RTE5 search pilot. In *Proc. of TAC*.

Debarghya Majumdar and Pushpak Bhattacharyya. 2010. Lexical based text entailment system for main task of RTE6. In *Proc. of TAC*.

Shachar Mirkin, Roy Bar-Haim, Jonathan Berant, Ido Dagan, Eyal Shnarch, Asher Stern, and Idan Szpektor. 2009a. Addressing discourse and document structure in the RTE search task. In *Proc. of TAC*.

Shachar Mirkin, Ido Dagan, and Eyal Shnarch. 2009b. Evaluating the inferential utility of lexical-semantic resources. In *Proc. of EACL*.

Judea Pearl. 1988. *Probabilistic reasoning in intelligent systems: networks of plausible inference*. Morgan Kaufmann.

Eyal Shnarch, Jacob Goldberger, and Ido Dagan. 2011. A probabilistic modeling framework for lexical entailment. In *Proc. of ACL*, pages 558–563.

Idan Szpektor, Ido Dagan, Roy Bar-Haim, and Jacob Goldberger. 2008. Contextual preferences. In *Proc. of ACL-08: HLT*.

Marta Tatu and Dan Moldovan. 2007. COGEX at RTE 3. In *Proc. of the ACL-PASCAL Workshop on Textual Entailment and Paraphrasing*.

Rui Wang, Yi Zhang, and Guenter Neumann. 2009. A joint syntactic-semantic representation for recognizing textual relatedness. In *Proc. of TAC*.

Fabio Massimo Zanzotto and Alessandro Moschitti. 2006. Automatic learning of textual entailments with cross-pair similarities. In *Proc. of ACL*.

A Appendix: An Iterative Procedure to Maximize $Q(\theta_{NA})$

There is no close-form expression for the parameter value θ_{NA} that maximizes expression (8) from Section 4.3. Instead we can apply the following iterative procedure. The derivative of $Q(\theta_{NA})$ is:

$$\frac{dQ(\theta_{NA})}{d\theta_{NA}} = \sum \left(\frac{l \cdot w_{hNA}}{\theta_{NA}} - \frac{(1-w_{hNA}) l \cdot \theta_{NA}^{(l-1)}}{1-\theta_{NA}^{l}} \right)$$

where $\frac{1}{l}$ is the hypothesis length and the summation is over all terms h in the training set. Setting this derivative to zero yields an equation which the optimal value satisfies:

$$\theta_{NA} = \frac{\sum l \cdot w_{hNA}}{\sum \frac{(1-w_{hNA}) l \cdot \theta_{NA}^{(l-1)}}{1-\theta_{NA}^{l}}} \quad (9)$$

Eq. (9) can be utilized as a heuristic iterative procedure to find the optimal value of θ_{NA}:

$$\theta_{NA} \leftarrow \frac{\sum l \cdot w_{hNA}}{\sum \frac{(1-w_{hNA}) l \cdot \theta_{NA}^{(l-1)}}{1-\theta_{NA}^{l}}}$$

Classification-based Contextual Preferences

Shachar Mirkin, Ido Dagan, Lili Kotlerman
Bar-Ilan University
Ramat Gan, Israel
{mirkins,dagan,davidol}@cs.biu.ac.il

Idan Szpektor
Yahoo! Research
Haifa, Israel
idan@yahoo-inc.com

Abstract

This paper addresses context matching in textual inference. We formulate the task under the *Contextual Preferences* framework which broadly captures contextual aspects of inference. We propose a generic classification-based scheme under this framework which coherently attends to context matching in inference and may be employed in any inference-based task. As a test bed for our scheme we use the Name-based Text Categorization (TC) task. We define an integration of Contextual Preferences into the TC setting and present a concrete self-supervised model which instantiates the generic scheme and is applied to address context matching in the TC task. Experiments on standard TC datasets show that our approach outperforms the state of the art in context modeling for Name-based TC.

1 Introduction

Textual inference is prevalent in text understanding applications. For example, in Question Answering (QA) the expected answer should be inferred from retrieved passages, and in Information Extraction (IE) the meaning of the target event is inferred from its mention in the text.

Lexical inferences make a substantial part of the inference process. In such cases, a target term is inferred from text expressions based on either one of two types of lexical matches: (i) a *direct match* of the target term in the text. For instance, the IE event injure may be detected by finding the word *injure* in the text; (ii) an *indirect match*, through a term that implies the meaning of the target term, e.g. inferring *injure* from *hurt*.

In either case, due to word ambiguity, it is necessary to validate that the context of the match conforms with the intended meaning of the target term before carrying out an inference operation based on this match. For example, "*You hurt my feelings*" constitutes an invalid context for the injure event as *hurt* in this text does not refer to a physical injury. Similarly, inferring the protest-related event demonstrate based on *demo* is deemed invalid although *demo* implies the meaning of the word *demonstrate* in other contexts, e.g., concerning *software demonstration*.

Although seemingly equivalent, a closer look reveals that the above two examples correspond to two distinct contextual mismatch situations. While the match of *hurt* is invalid for injure in the particular given context, an inference based on *demo* is invalid for the protest demonstrate event in any context.

Thus, several types of context matching are involved in textual inference. While most prior work addressed only specific context matching scenarios, Szpektor et al. (2008) presented a broader view, proposing a generic framework for context matching in inference, termed Contextual Preferences (CP). CP specifies the types of context matching that need to be considered in inference, allowing a model of choice to be applied for validating each type of match. Szpektor et al. applied CP to an IE task using different models to validate each type of context match.

In this work we adopt CP as our context matching framework and propose a novel classification-based scheme which provides unified modeling for CP. We represent typical contexts of the textual objects that participate in inference using classifiers; at inference time, each match is assessed by the respective classifiers which determine its contextual validity.

As a test bed we applied our scheme to the task

of Name-based Text Categorization. This is an unsupervised setting of TC where the only input given is the category name, and in which context validation is of high importance. We instantiate the scheme with a novel self-supervised model and apply it to the TC task. We suggest a method for integrating any CP-based context matching model into TC and use it to combine the context matching scores generated by our model. Results on two standard TC datasets show that our approach outperforms the state of the art context model for this task and suggest applying this scheme to additional inference-based applications.

2 Background

2.1 Context matching in inference

Word ambiguity has been traditionally addressed through Word Sense Disambiguation (WSD) (Navigli, 2009). The WSD task requires selecting the meaning of a target term from amongst a predefined set of senses, based on sense-inventories such as WordNet (Fellbaum, 1998).

An alternative approach eliminates the reliance on such inventories. Instead of explicit sense identification, a direct sense-match between terms is pursued (Dagan et al., 2006). *Lexical substitution* (McCarthy and Navigli, 2009) is probably the most commonly known task that follows this approach. *Context matching* is a generalization of lexical substitution, which seeks a match between terms in context, not necessarily for the purpose of substitution. For instance, the word *played* in "*U2 played their first-ever concert in Russia*" contextually matches *music*, although *music* cannot substitute *played* in this context. The context matching task, therefore, is to determine (by quantifying or giving a binary decision) the validity of a match between two terms in context.

In Section 1 we informally presented two cases of contextual mismatches. A comprehensive view of context matching types is provided by the Contextual Preferences framework (Szpektor et al., 2008). CP is phrased in terms of the Textual Entailment (TE) paradigm (Dagan et al., 2009). In TE, a *text t entails* a textual *hypothesis* h if the meaning of h can be inferred from t. Formulating the IE example from Section 1 within TE, h may be the name of the target event, *injure*, and t is a text segment from which h can be inferred. A direct match occurs when a term in h is identical to a term in t. An inference based on an indirect match is viewed as the application of a *lexical entailment rule*, r, such as '*hurt* $\Rightarrow$ *injure*', where the entailing left-hand side (LHS) of the rule (*hurt*) is matched in the text, while the entailed right-hand side (RHS), *injure*, is matched in the hypothesis.

Hence, three *inference objects* take part in inference operations: t, h and r. Most prior work addressed only specific contextual matches between these objects. For example, Harabagiu et al. (2003) matched the contexts of t and h for QA (answer and question, respectively); Barak et al. (2009) matched t and h (document and category) in TC, while other works, including those applying lexical substitution, typically validated the context match between t and r (Kauchak and Barzilay, 2006; Dagan et al., 2006; Pantel et al., 2007; Connor and Roth, 2007).

In comparison, in the CP framework, all possible contextual matches among t, h and r are considered: $t-h$, $t-r$ and $r-h$. The three context matches are depicted in Figure 1 (left). In CP, the representation of each inference object is enriched with contextual information which is used to characterize its valid contexts. Such information may be the words of the event description in IE, corpus instances based on which a rule was learned, or an annotation of relevant WordNet senses in Name-based TC. For example, a category name hockey may be assigned with the sense number corresponding to *ice hockey*, but not to *field hockey*, in order to designate information that limits the valid contexts of the category to the former among the two meanings of the name.

Before an inference operation is performed, the context representations of each pair among the participating objects should be *matched* by a context model in order to assess the contextual validity of the operation. Along with the context representation and the specific context matching models, the way context model decisions are combined needs to be specified in a concrete implementation of the CP framework.

2.2 Context matching models

Several approaches were taken in prior work to model context matching, mostly within the scope of learning *selectional preferences* of templatized lexical-syntactic rules (e.g. '$X \xleftarrow{subj} hit \xrightarrow{obj} Y$' $\Rightarrow$ '$X \xleftarrow{subj} attack \xrightarrow{obj} Y$').

Pantel et al. (2007) and Szpektor et al. (2008) represented the context of such rules as the intersection of preferences of the rule's LHS and RHS, namely the observed argument instantiations or their semantic classes. A rule is deemed applicable to a given text if the argument instantiations in the text are similar to the selectional preferences of the rule. To overcome sparseness, other works represented context in latent space. Pennacchiotti et al. (2007) and Szpektor et al. (2008) measured the similarity between the Latent Semantic Analysis (LSA) (Deerwester et al., 1990) representations of matched contexts. Dinu and Lapata (2010) used Latent Dirichlet Allocation (LDA) (Blei et al., 2003) to model templates' latent senses, determining rule applicability based on the similarity between the two sides of the rule when instantiated by the context, while Ritter et al. (2010) used LDA to model argument classes, considering a rule valid for a given argument instantiation if its instantiated templates are drawn from the same hidden topic.

A different approach is provided by classification-based models which learn classifiers for inference objects. A classifier is trained based on positive and negative examples which represent valid or invalid contexts of the object; from those, features characterizing the context are extracted, e.g. words in a window around the target term or syntactic links with it. Given a new context, the classifier assesses its validity with respect to the learned classification model.

Classifiers in prior work were applied to determine rule applicability in a given context ($t - r$). Training a classifier for word paraphrasing, Kauchak and Barzilay (2006) used occurrences of the rule's RHS as positive context examples, and randomly picked negative examples. A similar approach was applied by Dagan et al. (2006), which used a single-class SVM to avoid selecting negative examples. In both works, a resulting classifier represents a word with all its senses intermixed. Clearly, this poses no problem for monosemous words, but is biased towards the more common senses of polysemous words. Indeed, Dagan et al. (2006) report a negative correlation between the degree of polysemy of a word and the performance of its classifier. Connor and Roth (2007) used per-rule classifiers to produce a noisy training set for learning a global classifier for verb substitution.

In this work we follow the classification-based approach which seems appealing for several reasons.

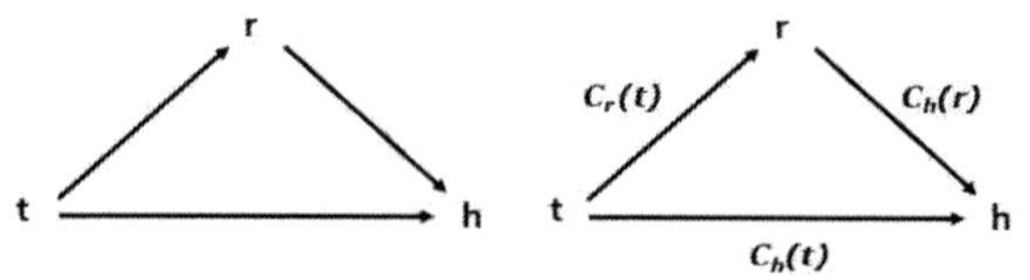

Figure 1: Left: An illustration of the CP relationships as in (Szpektor et al., 2008), with arrows indicting the context matching direction; Right: The application of classifiers to the tested contexts under our scheme.

First, it allows seamlessly integrating various types of information via classifiers' features; unlike some of the above models, it is not inherently dependent on the type of rules that are utilized and easily accommodates to both lexical and lexical-syntactic rules through the choice of features. In addition, it does not rely on a predefined similarity measure and provides flexibility in terms of model's parameters. Finally, this approach captures the notion of directionality which is fundamental in textual inference, and is therefore better suited to applied inference than previously proposed symmetric context models.

In comparison to prior classification-based models, our approach addresses all three context matches specified by CP, rather than only the rule-text match. It is not limited to substitutable terms or even to terms with the same part of speech. In addition, we avoid learning a classifier for all senses combined, but rather learn it for the specific intended meaning.

2.3 Name-based Text Categorization

Name-based TC (Gliozzo et al., 2009) is an unsupervised setting of Text Categorization in which the only input provided is the category name, e.g. trade, 'mergers and acquisitions' or guns. When category names are ambiguous, e.g. space, categories are not well defined; thus, auxiliary information is expected to accompany the name for disambiguation, such as a list of relevant senses or a category description.

Typically, unsupervised TC consists of two steps. First, an unsupervised method is applied to an unlabeled corpus, automatically labeling some of the documents to categories. Then, the labeled documents from the first step are used to train a supervised TC classifier which is used to label any document in the test set (Gliozzo et al., 2009; Downey and Etzioni, 2009; Barak et al., 2009).

In this work we focus on the above unsupervised step. Gliozzo et al. (2009) addressed this task by representing both documents and categories by LSA vectors which implicitly capture contextual similarities between terms. Each document was then assigned to the most similar category based on cosine similarity between the LSA vectors. Barak et al. (2009) required an occurrence of a term entailing the category name (or the category name itself) in order to regard the category as a candidate for the document. To assess the contextual validity of the match, they used LSA document-category similarity as in (Gliozzo et al., 2009). For example, to classify a document into the category medicine, at least one lexical entailment rule, e.g. '*drug* ⇒ *medicine*', should be matched in the document. Then, the validity of *drug* for medicine in the matched document is assessed by the LSA context model. In this work we adopt Barak et al.'s requirement for a match for the category in the document, but address context matching in an entirely different way.

Name-based TC provides a convenient setting for evaluating context matching approaches for two main reasons. First, all types of context matchings are realized in this application (see Section 3); second, as the hypothesis consists of a single term or a few terms, the TC gold standard annotation corresponds quite directly to the context matching task for lexical inferences; in other applications where longer hypotheses are involved, context matching performance may be masked by other factors.

3 Contextual Matches in TC

Within Name-based TC, the Textual Entailment terminology is mapped as follows: h is a term denoting the category name (e.g. *merger* or *acquisition*); t is a matched term in the document to be categorized from which h may be inferred; and a match refers to an occurrence in the document of either h (direct match) or the LHS of an entailment rule r whose RHS is a category name (indirect match).[1]

Under the CP view, a context model needs to address the following three context matching cases within a TC setting.

$t-h$: Assessing the validity of a match in the document with respect to the category's intended meaning. For example, the occurrence of the category name space (in the sense of *outer space*) in "*the server ran out of disk space*" does not indicate a space-related text, and should be dismissed by the context model.

$t-r$: This case refers to a rule match in the document. A context model should ensure that the meaning of a match is compatible with that of the rule. For example, '*alien* ⇒ *space*' is a valid rule for the space category. Yet, it should not be applied to "*The US welcomes a large number of aliens every year*", since *alien* in this sentence has a different meaning than the intended meaning of the rule.

$r-h$: The match between the intended meanings of the category name and the RHS of the rule. For instance, the rule '*room* ⇒ *space*' is not suitable at all for the (outer) space category.

4 A Classification-based Scheme for CP

Szpektor et al. (2008) introduced a vector-space model to implement CP, in which the text t, the rule r and the hypothesis h share the same contextual representation. However, in CP, r, h and t have non-symmetric roles: the context of t should be tested as valid for r and h and not vice versa, and the context of r should be validated for h and not the other way around. This stems from the need to consider directionality in context matching. For instance, a text about *football* typically constitutes a valid context for the more general *sports* context, but not vice versa. Indeed, directionality may be captured in vector-space models by using a directional similarity measure (Kotlerman et al., 2010), but only symmetric measures were used in context matching work so far.

Based on this distinction between the inference objects' roles, we present a novel scheme that uses two types of classifiers to represent context:

C_h: A classifier that identifies valid contexts for h. It tests contexts of t (for $t-h$ matching) or r (for $r-h$ matching), assigning them scores $C_h(t)$ and $C_h(r)$, respectively.

C_r: A classifier that identifies valid contexts for applying the rule r. It tests the context of t, assigning it a score $C_r(t)$.

Figure 1 (right) shows the classifiers scores which are assigned to each of the matching types.

[1]Note that t and h both refer here to individual terms.

Hence, h always acts as the *classifying object*, t is always the *classified object*, while r acts as both. Context matching is quantified by the degree by which the classified object represents a valid context for the classifying object in a given inference scenario.

In comparison to the CP implementation in (Szpektor et al., 2008), our approach uses a unified model which captures directionality in context matching.

To instantiate the scheme, one needs to define the way training examples are obtained and processed. This may be done within supervised classification, where labeled examples are provided, or – as we do in this work – using self-supervised classifiers which obtain training examples automatically. We present such an instantiation in Section 5, where a classifier is trained for each category and each rule. When more complex hypotheses are involved, C_h classifiers can be trained separately for each relevant part of the hypothesis, using the rest for disambiguation.

A combination of the three model scores provides a final context matching score. In Section 6 we suggest a way to combine the actual classification scores as part of the integration of CP into TC, but other combinations are plausible. In particular, binary classifications (valid vs. invalid) may be used as filters. That is, the context is classified as valid only if all relevant models classify it as such.

5 A Self-supervised Context Model

We now turn to demonstrate how our classification-based scheme may be implemented. The model below is exemplified on Name-based TC, but may be applicable to other tasks, with few changes.

5.1 Training-set generation

Our implementation is self-supervised as we want to integrate it within the unsupervised TC setting. That is, the classifiers automatically obtain training examples for the classifying object (a category or a rule) without relying on labeled documents.

We obtain examples by querying the TC training corpus with automatically-generated search queries. The difficulty lies in correctly constructing queries that will retrieve documents representing either valid or invalid contexts for the classifying object. To this end, we retrieve examples through a gradual process in which the most accurate (least ambiguous) query is used first and less accurate queries follow, until the designated number of examples is acquired.

5.1.1 Obtaining positive examples

To acquire positive training examples, we construct queries which are comprised of two main clauses. The first contains the *seeds*, terms which characterize the classifying object. Primarily, these are the category name or the LHS of the rule. The second consists of *context words* which are used when the seeds are polysemous, and are intended to assist disambiguation. When context words are used, at least one seed and at least one context word must be matched to retrieve a document. For example, given the highly ambiguous category name space, we first construct the query using only the monosemous term *outer space*; if the number of retrieved documents does not meet the requirement, a second query may be constructed: *("outer space"* OR *space)* AND *(infinite* OR *science* OR ... *)*.

To generate a rule classifier C_r, we retrieve positive examples as follows. If the LHS term is monosemous according to WordNet[2], we first query using this term alone (e.g. *decrypt*), and add its monosemous synonyms and hyponyms if more examples are required (e.g. *decrypt* OR *decode*). If the LHS is polysemous, we carry out Procedure 1. Intuitively, this procedure tries to minimize ambiguity by using monosemous terms as much as possible; when polysemous terms must be used, it tries to ensure there are monosemous terms to disambiguate them. Note that entailment directionality is maintained throughout the process, as seeds are only expanded with more specific (entailing) terms, while context words are only expanded with more general (entailed) terms.

Procedure 1 : Retrieval of C_r positive examples

Apply sequentially until sufficient examples are obtained:

1: Set the LHS as seed and the RHS's monosemous synonyms, hypernyms and derivations as context words.
2: Add monosemous synonyms and hyponyms of the LHS to the seeds.
3: As in 2, but use polysemous terms as well.
4: Add polysemous context words.

Positive examples for category classifiers (C_h) are obtained through a similar procedure as for rule clas-

[2]Terms not in WordNet are assumed monosemous.

sifiers. If the category is part of a hierarchy, we also use the name of the parent category (e.g. *sport* for rec.sport.hockey) as a context word.

5.1.2 Obtaining negative examples

Negative examples are even more challenging to acquire. In prior work negative examples were selected randomly (Kauchak and Barzilay, 2006; Connor and Roth, 2007). We follow this method, but also attempt to identify negative examples that are semantically similar to the positive ones in order to improve the discriminative power of the classifier (Smith and Eisner, 2005). We do that by applying a similar procedure which uses cohyponyms of the seeds, e.g. *baseball* for hockey or *islam* for christianity. Cohyponymy is a non-entailing relation; hence, by using it we expect to obtain semantically-related, yet invalid contexts. If not enough negative examples are retrieved using cohyponyms, we select the remaining required examples randomly.

As the distribution of positive and negative examples in the data is unknown, we set the ratio of negative to positive examples as a parameter of the model, as in (Bergsma et al., 2008).

5.1.3 Insufficient examples

When the number of training examples for a rule or a category is below a certain minimum, the resulting classifier is expected to be of poor quality. This usually happens for positive examples in any of the following two cases: (i) the seed is rare in the training set; (ii) the desired sense of the seed is rarely found in the training set, and unwanted senses were filtered by our retrieval query. For instance, *nazarene* does not occur at all in the training set, and the classifier corresponding to the rule '*nazarene* $\Rightarrow$ *christian*' cannot be generated. On the other hand, *cone* does appear in the corpus but not in the astrophysical sense the rule '*cone* $\Rightarrow$ *space*' refers to. In such cases we refrain from generating the classifier and use instead a default score of 0 for each classified object. The idea is that rare terms will also occur infrequently in the test set, while cases where the term is found in the corpus, but in a different sense than the desired one, will be blocked.

5.1.4 Feature extraction

We extract global and local lexical features that are standard in WSD work. Global features include all the terms in the document or in the sentence in which a match was found. Local features are extracted around matches of seeds which comprised the query that retrieved the document. These features include the terms in a window around the match, and the noun, verb, adjective and adverb nearest to the match in either direction. For randomly sampled negative examples, where no matched query terms exist, we randomly select terms in the document as "matches" for local feature extraction. If more than one match of the same term is found in a document, we assume one-sense-per-discourse (Gale et al., 1992) and jointly extract features for all matches of the term.

5.2 Applying the classifiers

During inference, for each direct match in a document, the corresponding C_h is applied. For an indirect match, the respective C_r is also applied.

In addition, C_h is applied to the matched rules. Unlike t, a rule is not represented by a single text. Therefore, to test a rule's match with the category, we randomly sample from the training set documents containing the rule's LHS. We apply C_h to each sampled example and compute the ratio of positive classifications. The result is a score indicating the domain-specific probability of the rule to be applicable to the category, and may be interpreted as an in-domain *prior*. For instance, the rule '*check* $\Rightarrow$ *hockey*' is assigned a score of 0.05, since the sense of *check* as a hockey defense technique is rare in the corpus. On the other hand, non ambiguous rules, e.g. '*warship* $\Rightarrow$ *ship*' are assigned a high probability (1.0), and so are rules whose LHS is ambiguous but its dominant sense in the training corpus is the same one the rule refers to, e.g. '*margin* $\Rightarrow$ *earnings*'(0.85).

We do not assign negative classifier scores to invalid matches but rather set them to zero instead. The reason is that an invalid context only indicates that the term cannot be used for entailing the category name, but not that the document itself is irrelevant.

6 CP for Text Categorization

CP may be employed in any inference-based task, but the integration with each task is somewhat different and needs to be specified. Below we present a methodology for integrating CP into Name-based Text Categorization.

As in (Barak et al., 2009) (*Barak09* below), we represent documents and categories by term-vectors in the following way: a document vector contains the document terms; a category vector contains two sets of terms: $\mathcal{C}$, the terms denoting the category name, and $\mathcal{E}$, their entailing terms. For example, *oil* is added to the vector of the category crude by the rule '*oil* $\Rightarrow$ *crude*' (i.e. *crude* $\in \mathcal{C}$ and *oil* $\in \mathcal{E}$).

Barak09 assigned equal values of 1 to all vector entries. We suggest integrating a CP-based context model into TC by re-weighting the terms in the vectors, prior to determining the final document-category categorization score through vector similarity. Given a category c, with term vector C, and a document d with term vector D, the model re-weights vector entries of matching terms (i.e., terms in $C \cap D$), based on the validity of the context match. Valid matches should be assigned with higher scores than invalid ones, leading to higher overall vector similarity for documents with valid matches for the given category. Non-matching terms are ignored as their weights are canceled out in the subsequent vector product.

Specifically, the model assigns a new weight $w_D(u)$ to a matching term u in the document vector D based on the model's assessment of: (a) $t - h$, the context match between the (match in the) document and the category; and (if an indirect match) (b) $t - r$, the context match between the document and the rule '$u \Rightarrow c_i$', where $c_i \in \mathcal{C}$. The model also sets a new weight $w_C(v)$ to a term v in the category vector C based on the context match for $r - h$, between the rule '$v \Rightarrow c_j$' ($c_j \in \mathcal{C}$) and the category. For instance, using our context matching scheme in TC, $w_D(u)$ is set to $C_h(u)$ or $\frac{C_h(u)+C_r(u)}{2}$ for direct and indirect matches, respectively; $w_C(v)$ is left as 1 if $v \in \mathcal{C}$ and set to $C_h(v)$ when $v \in \mathcal{E}$.

Barak09 assigned a single global context score to a document-category pair using the LSA representations of their vectors. In our approach, however, we consider the actual matches from the three different views, hence the re-weighting of the vector entries using three model scores.

7 Experimental Setting

7.1 Datasets and knowledge resources

Following (Gliozzo et al., 2009) and (Barak et al., 2009), we evaluated our method on two standard TC datasets: *Reuters-10* and *20-Newsgroups*.

The *Reuters-10* (R10, for short) is a sub-corpus of the Reuters-21578 collection[3], constructed from the ten most frequent categories in the Reuters taxonomy. We used the Apte split of the Reuters-21578 collection, often used in TC tasks. The top 10 categories include about 9,000 documents, split into training (70%) and test (30%) sets. The *20-Newsgroups* (20NG) corpus is a collection of newsgroup postings gathered from twenty different categories from the Usenet Newsgroups hierarchy[4]. We used the "by-date" version of the corpus, which contains approximately 20,000 documents partitioned (nearly) evenly across the categories and divided in advance to training (60%) and test (40%) sets.

As in (Gliozzo et al., 2009; Barak et al., 2009), we adjusted non-standard category names (e.g. forsale was renamed to sale) and manually specified for each category its relevant WordNet senses. The sense tagging properly defines the categories, and is expected to accompany such hypotheses. Other types of information may be used for this purpose, e.g. words from category descriptions, if such exist.

We applied standard preprocessing (sentence splitting, tokenization, lemmatization and part of speech tagging) to all documents in the datasets. All terms, including those denoting category names and rules, are represented by their lemma and part of speech.

As sources for lexical entailment rules we used WordNet 3.0 (synonyms, hyponyms, derivations and meronyms) and a Wikipedia-derived rule-base (Shnarch et al., 2009). Unlike *Barak09* we did not limit the rules extracted from WordNet to the most frequent senses and used all rule types from the Wikipedia-based resource.

7.2 Self-supervised model tuning

Tuning of the self-supervised context model's parameters (number of training examples, negative to positive ratio, feature set and the way negative examples are obtained) was performed over development sets sampled from the training sets. Based on this tuning, some parameters varied between the datasets and between classifier types (C_h vs. C_r). For example,

[3]http://kdd.ics.uci.edu/databases/reuters21578/reuters21578.html

[4]http://people.csail.mit.edu/jrennie/20Newsgroups/

selection of negative examples based on cohyponyms was found useful for C_r classifiers in R10, while random examples were used in the rest of the cases.

We used *SVM^{perf}* (Joachims, 2006) with a linear kernel and binary feature weighting.

For querying the corpus we used the Lucene search engine[5] in its default setting. Up to 150 positive examples were retrieved for each classifier, with 5 examples set as the required minimum. This resulted in generating 100% of the hypothesis classifiers for both datasets and 95% and 70% of the rule classifiers for R10 and 20NG, respectively.

We computed $C_h(r)$ scores based on up to 20 sampled instances. If less than 2 examples were found in the training set, we assigned an "unknown" context match probability of 0.5, since a rare LHS occurrence does not indicate anything about its meaning in the corpus. Such cases constituted 2% (R10) and 11% (20NG) of the utilized rules.

7.3 Baseline models

To provide a more meaningful comparison with prior work, we focus on the first unsupervised step in the typical Name-based TC flow, without the subsequent supervised training. Our goal is to improve the accuracy of this first step, and we therefore compare our context model's performance to two unsupervised methods used by *Barak09*.

The first baseline, denoted *Barak$_{no\text{-}cxt}$*, is the cosine similarity score between the document and category vectors where all terms are equally weighted to a score of 1.[6] This baseline shows the performance when no context model is employed.

The second baseline, denoted *Barak$_{full}$*, is a replication of the state of the art context model for Name-based TC. In this method, LSA vectors are constructed for a document by averaging the LSA vectors of its individual terms, and for a category by averaging the LSA vectors of the terms denoting its name. The categorization score of a document-category pair is set to be the product between the cosine similarity score of the LSA vectors and the score given by the above *Barak$_{no\text{-}cxt}$* method. We note that LSA-based context models performed best also in (Gliozzo et al., 2009) and (Szpektor et al., 2008).

[5] `http://lucene.apache.org`

[6] Other attempted weighting schemes, such as tf-idf, did not yield better performance.

Model	Reuters-10			
	Accuracy	P	R	F_1
Barak$_{no\text{-}cxt}$	73.2	63.6	77.0	69.7
Barak$_{full}$	76.3	68.0	79.2	73.2
Class.-based	**79.3**	**71.8**	**83.6**	**77.2**

Model	20-Newsgroups			
	Accuracy	P	R	F_1
Barak$_{no\text{-}cxt}$	63.7	44.5	74.6	55.8
Barak$_{full}$	69.4	50.1	**82.8**	62.4
Class.-based	**73.4**	**54.7**	76.4	**63.7**

Table 1: Evaluation results.

All models were constructed based on the TC training sets, using no external corpora. The vocabulary consists of terms that appear more than once in the training set. The terms we consider include nouns, verbs, adjectives and adverbs, as well as nominal multi-word expressions.

8 Results and Analysis

Given a document, all categories for which a lexical match was found in the document are considered, and the document is classified to the highest scoring category. If all categories are assigned non-positive scores, the document is not assigned to any of them.

Based on this requirement that a document contains at least one match for the category, 4862 document-category pairs were considered for classification in R10 and 9955 pairs in 20NG. We evaluated our context model, as well as the baselines, based on the *accuracy* of these classifications, i.e. the percentage of correct decisions among the candidate document-category pairs. We also measured the models' performance in terms of micro-averaged *precision (P)*, *relative recall (R)* and F_1. Like *Barak09*, recall is computed relative to the potential recall of the rule-set which provides the entailing terms.

Table 1 presents the evaluation results. As in *Barak09*, the LSA-based model outperforms the first baseline, supporting its usefulness as a context model. In both datasets our model outperformed the baselines in terms of accuracy. This result is statistically significant with $p < 0.01$ according to McNemar's test (McNemar, 1947). Recall is lower for our model in 20NG but F_1 scores are higher for both datasets. These results indicate that the classification-based context model provides a favorable alternative to the

Removed	*Reuters-10*		*20-Newsgroups*	
	Accuracy	F_1	Accuracy	F_1
-	79.3	77.2	73.4	63.7
$C_h(t)$	76.2	72.3	71.9	61.0
$C_r(t)$	80.5	77.6	74.3	64.5
$C_h(r)$	78.4	75.7	73.1	63.4

Table 2: Ablation tests results.

state of the art LSA-based method.

Table 2 presents ablation tests of our model. In each test we measured the classification performance when one of the three classification scores is ignored. Clearly, $C_h(t)$ is the most beneficial component, and in general the category classifiers help improving overall performance. The limited performance of C_r may be related to higher ambiguity in rules relative to category names, resulting in noisier training data. In addition, the small size of the training set limits the number of training examples for rule classifiers. This problem affects C_r more than C_h since, by nature, the corpus includes more occurrences of category names. Still, C_r contributes to improved recall (this fact is not visible in Table 2).

The coverage of the utilized rule-set determines the maximal (absolute) recall that can be achieved by any model. With the rule-set we used in this experiment, the recall upper bound was 59.1% for R10 and 40.6% for 20NG. However, rule coverage affects precision as well: In many cases documents are assigned to incorrect categories because the correct category is not even a candidate as no entailing term was matched for it in the document. For instance, a document with the sentence *"For sale or trade!!! BMW R60US..."* was classified by our method to the category forsale, while its gold-standard category is motorcycles. Yet, none of the rules in our rule-set triggered motorcycles as a candidate category for this document. Ideally, a context model would rule out all incorrect candidate categories; in practice even a single low score for one of the competing categories results in a false positive error in such cases (in addition to the recall loss). To reduce these problems we intend to employ additional knowledge resources in future work.

Our algorithm for retrieving training examples turned out to be not sufficiently accurate, particularly for negative examples. This is a challenging task that requires further research. Although useful for some classifier types, the use of cohyponyms may retrieve potentially positive examples as negative ones, since terms that are considered cohyponyms in WordNet are often perceived as near synonyms in common usage, e.g. *buyout* and *purchase* in the context of acquisitions. Likewise, using WordNet senses to determine ambiguity is also inaccurate. Rare or too fine-grained senses, common in WordNet, cause a term to be considered ambiguous, which in turn triggers the use of less accurate retrieval methods. For example, *auction* has a bridge-related WordNet sense which is irrelevant for our dataset, but made the term be considered ambiguous. This calls for development of other methods for determining word ambiguity, which consider the actual usage of terms in the domain rather than relying solely on WordNet.

9 Conclusions

In this paper we presented a generic classification-based scheme for comprehensively addressing context matching in textual inference scenarios. We presented a concrete implementation of the proposed scheme for Name-based TC, and showed how CP decisions can be integrated within the TC setting.

Utilizing classifiers for context matching offers several advantages. They naturally incorporate directionality and allow integrating various types of information, including ones not used in this work such as syntactic features. Our results indeed support this approach. Still, further research is required regarding issues raised by the use of multiple classifiers, scalability in particular.

Hypotheses in TC are available in advance. While also the case in other applications, it constitutes a practical challenge when hypotheses are given "online", like Information Retrieval queries, since classifiers will have to be generated on the fly. We intend to address this issue in future work.

Lastly, we plan to apply the generic classification-based approach to address context matching in other inference-based applications.

Acknowledgments

This work was partially supported by the Israel Science Foundation grant 1112/08 and the NEGEV project (`www.negev-initiative.org`).

References

Libby Barak, Ido Dagan, and Eyal Shnarch. 2009. Text Categorization from Category Name via Lexical Reference. In *HLT-NAACL (Short Papers)*.

Shane Bergsma, Dekang Lin, and Randy Goebel. 2008. Discriminative Learning of Selectional Preference from Unlabeled Text. In *In Proceedings of EMNLP*.

David M. Blei, Andrew Y. Ng, and Michael I. Jordan. 2003. Latent Dirichlet Allocation. *Journal of Machine Learning Research*, 3:993–1022, March.

Michael Connor and Dan Roth. 2007. Context Sensitive Paraphrasing with a Global Unsupervised Classifier. In *Proceedings of ECML*.

Ido Dagan, Oren Glickman, Alfio Gliozzo, Efrat Marmorshtein, and Carlo Strapparava. 2006. Direct Word Sense Matching for Lexical Substitution. In *Proceedings of COLING-ACL*.

Ido Dagan, Bill Dolan, Bernardo Magnini, and Dan Roth. 2009. Recognizing Textual Entailment: Rational, Evaluation and Approaches. *Natural Language Engineering*, pages 15(4):1–17.

Scott Deerwester, Scott Deerwester, Susan T. Dumais, George W. Furnas, Thomas K. Landauer, and Richard Harshman. 1990. Indexing by Latent Semantic Analysis. *Journal of the American Society for Information Science*, 41:391–407.

Georgiana Dinu and Mirella Lapata. 2010. Topic Models for Meaning Similarity in Context. In *Proceedings of Coling 2010: Posters*.

Doug Downey and Oren Etzioni. 2009. Look Ma, No Hands: Analyzing the Monotonic Feature Abstraction for Text Classification. In *Proceedings of NIPS*.

Christiane Fellbaum, editor. 1998. *WordNet: An Electronic Lexical Database (Language, Speech, and Communication)*. The MIT Press.

William A. Gale, Kenneth W. Church, and David Yarowsky. 1992. One Sense per Discourse. In *Proceedings of the workshop on Speech and Natural Language*.

Alfio Gliozzo, Carlo Strapparava, and Ido Dagan. 2009. Improving Text Categorization Bootstrapping via Unsupervised Learning. *ACM Trans. Speech Lang. Process.*, 6:1:1–1:24, October.

Sanda M. Harabagiu, Steven J. Maiorano, and Marius A. Paşca. 2003. Open-domain Textual Question Answering Techniques. *Natural Language Engineering*, 9:231–267, September.

Thorsten Joachims. 2006. Training Linear SVMs in Linear Time. In *Proceedings of the ACM Conference on Knowledge Discovery and Data Mining (KDD)*.

David Kauchak and Regina Barzilay. 2006. Paraphrasing for Automatic Evaluation. In *Proceedings of HLT-NAACL*.

Lili Kotlerman, Ido Dagan, Idan Szpektor, and Maayan Zhitomirsky-Geffet. 2010. Directional Distributional Similarity for Lexical Inference. *Natural Language Engineering*, 16(4):359–389.

Diana McCarthy and Roberto Navigli. 2009. The English Lexical Substitution Task. *Language Resources and Evaluation*, 43(2):139–159.

Quinn McNemar. 1947. Note on the Sampling Error of the Difference between Correlated Proportions or Percentages. *Psychometrika*, 12(2):153–157, June.

Roberto Navigli. 2009. Word Sense Disambiguation: A Survey. *ACM Computing Surveys*, 41(2):1–69.

Patrick Pantel, Rahul Bhagat, Bonaventura Coppola, Timothy Chklovski, and Eduard Hovy. 2007. ISP: Learning Inferential Selectional Preferences. In *Proceedings of NAACL-HLT*.

Marco Pennacchiotti, Roberto Basili, Diego De Cao, and Paolo Marocco. 2007. Learning Selectional Preferences for Entailment or Paraphrasing Rules. In *Proceedings of RANLP*.

Alan Ritter, Mausam, and Oren Etzioni. 2010. A Latent Dirichlet Allocation Method for Selectional Preferences. In *Proceedings of ACL*.

Eyal Shnarch, Libby Barak, and Ido Dagan. 2009. Extracting Lexical Reference Rules from Wikipedia. In *Proceedings of IJCNLP-ACL*.

Noah A. Smith and Jason Eisner. 2005. Contrastive Estimation: Training Log-linear Models on Unlabeled Data. In *Proceedings of ACL*.

Idan Szpektor, Ido Dagan, Roy Bar-Haim, and Jacob Goldberger. 2008. Contextual Preferences. In *Proceedings of ACL-08: HLT*.

Is it Worth Submitting this Run? Assess your RTE System with a Good Sparring Partner

Milen Kouylekov
CELI s.r.l.
Turin, Italy
kouylekov@celi.it

Yashar Mehdad
FBK-irst and University of Trento
Trento, Italy
mehdad@fbk.eu

Matteo Negri
FBK-irst
Trento, Italy
negri@fbk.eu

Abstract

We address two issues related to the development of systems for Recognizing Textual Entailment. The first is the impossibility to capitalize on lessons learned over the different datasets available, due to the changing nature of traditional RTE evaluation settings. The second is the lack of simple ways to assess the results achieved by our system on a given training corpus, and figure out its real potential on unseen test data. Our contribution is the extension of an open-source RTE package with an automatic way to explore the large search space of possible configurations, in order to select the most promising one over a given dataset. From the developers' point of view, the efficiency and ease of use of the system, together with the good results achieved on all previous RTE datasets, represent a useful support, providing an immediate term of comparison to position the results of their approach.

1 Introduction

Research on textual entailment (TE) has received a strong boost by the Recognizing Textual Entailment (RTE) Challenges, organized yearly to gather the community around a shared evaluation framework. Within such framework, besides the intrinsic difficulties of the task (*i.e.* deciding, given a set of *Text-Hypothesis* pairs, if the hypotheses can be inferred from the meaning of the texts), the development of RTE systems has to confront with a number of additional problems and uncertainty factors. First of all, since RTE systems are usually based on complex architectures that integrate a variety of tools and resources, it is *per se* very difficult to tune them and define the optimal configuration given a new dataset. In general, when participating to the evaluation challenges there's no warranty that the submitted runs are those obtained with the best possible configuration allowed by the system. Second, the evaluation settings change along the years. Variations in the length of the texts, the origin of the pairs, the balance between positive and negative examples, and the type of entailment decisions allowed, reflect the need to move from easier and more artificial settings to more complex and natural ones. However, in contrast with other more stable tasks in terms of evaluation settings and metrics (*e.g.* machine translation), such changes make it difficult to capitalize on the experience obtained by participants throughout the years. Third, looking at RTE-related literature and the outcomes of the six campaigns organised so far, the conclusions that can be drawn are often controversial. For instance, it is not clear whether the availability of larger amounts of training data correlates with better performance (Hickl et al., 2006) or not (Zanzotto et al., 2007; Hickl and Bensley, 2007), even within the same evaluation setting. In addition, ablation tests carried out in recent editions of the challenge do not allow for definite conclusions about the actual usefulness of tools and resources, even the most popular ones (Bentivogli et al., 2009). Finally, the best performing systems often have different natures from one year to another, showing alternations of deep (Hickl and Bensley, 2007; Tatu and Moldovan, 2007) and shallow approaches (Jia et al., 2010) ranked at the top positions. In light of these considerations, it would be useful for systems developers to have: *i)* automatic ways to support systems' tuning at a training stage, and *ii)* reliable terms of comparison to validate their hypotheses, and position the results of their work before submitting runs for evaluation. In this paper we address these needs by extending an open-source RTE package (EDITS[1]) with a mechanism that automatizes the selection of the most promising configuration over a training dataset. We prove the effectiveness of such extension showing that it allows not only to achieve good performance on all the available RTE Challenge datasets, but also to improve the official results, achieved with the same system, through *ad hoc* configurations manually defined by the developers team. Our contribution is twofold. On one side, in the spirit of the collaborative nature of open source projects, we extend an existing tool with a useful functionality that was still missing. On the other side, we provide a good "sparring partner" for system developers, to be used as a fast and free term of comparison to position the results of their work.

2 "Coping" with configurability

EDITS (Kouylekov and Negri, 2010) is an open source RTE package, which offers a modular, flexible, and adaptable working environment to experiment with the RTE task over different datasets. The package allows to: *i)* create an entailment engine by defining its basic components (i.e. algorithms, cost schemes, rules, and optimizers); *ii)* train such entailment engine over an annotated RTE corpus to learn a model; and *iii)* use the entailment engine and the model to assign an entailment judgement and a confidence score to each pair of an un-annotated test corpus. A key feature of EDITS is represented by its high configurability, allowed by the availability of different algorithms, the possibility to integrate different sets of lexical entailment/contradiction rules, and the variety of parameters for performance optimization (see also Mehdad, 2009). Although configurability is *per se* an important aspect (especially for an open-source and general purpose system), there is another side of the coin. In principle, in order to select the most promising configuration over a given development set, one should exhaustively run a huge number of training/evaluation routines. Such number corresponds to the total number of configurations allowed by the system, which result from the possible combinations of parameter settings. When dealing with enlarging dataset sizes, and the tight time constraints usually posed by the evaluation campaigns, this problem becomes particularly challenging, as developers are hardly able to run exhaustive training/evaluation routines. As recently shown by the EDITS developers team, such situation results in running a limited number of experiments with the most "reasonable" configurations, which consequently might not lead to the optimal solution (Kouylekov et al., 2010).

The need of a mechanism to automatically obtain the most promising solution on one side, and the constraints posed by the evaluation campaigns on the other side, arise the necessity to optimize this procedure. Along this direction, the objective is good a trade-off between exhaustive experimentation with all possible configurations (unfeasible), and educated guessing (unreliable). The remainder of this section tackles this issue introducing an optimization strategy based on genetic algorithms, and describing its adaptation to extend EDITS with the new functionality.

2.1 Genetic algorithm

Genetic algorithms (GA) are well suited to efficiently deal with large search spaces, and have been recently applied with success to a variety of optimization problems and specific NLP tasks (Figueroa and Neumann, 2008; Otto and Riff, 2004; Aycinena et al., 2003). GA are a direct stochastic method for global search and optimization, which mimics natural evolution. To this aim, they work with a *population of individuals*, representing possible solutions to the given task. Traditionally, solutions are represented in binary as strings of *0*s and *1*s, but other encodings (*e.g.* sequences of real values) are possible. The evolution usually starts from a population of randomly generated individuals, and at each generation selects the best-suited individuals based on a *fitness function* (which measures the optimality of the solution obtained by the individual). Such selection is then followed by *modifications* of the selected individuals obtained by recombining (crossover) and performing random changes (mutation) to form a new population, which will be used in the next iter-

[1] http://edits.fbk.eu/

ation. Finally, the algorithm is terminated when the maximum number of generations, or a satisfactory fitness level has been reached for the population.

2.2 EDITS-GA

Our extension to the EDITS package, EDITS-GA, consists in an iterative process that starts with an initial population of randomly generated configurations. After a training phase with the generated configurations, the process is evaluated by means of the fitness function, which is manually defined by the user[2]. This measure is used by the genetic algorithm to iteratively build new populations of configurations, which are trained and evaluated. This process can be seen as the combination of: *i)* a micro training/evaluation routine for each generated configuration of the entailment engine; and *ii)* a macro evolutionary cycle, as illustrated in Figure 1. The fitness function is an important factor for the evaluation and the evolution of the generated configurations, as it drives the evolutionary process by determining the best-suited individuals used to generate new populations. The procedure to estimate and optimize the best configuration applying the GA, can be summarized as follows.

(1) Initialization: generate a random initial population (*i.e.* a set of configurations).

(2) Selection:

2a. The fitness function (accuracy, or F-measure) is evaluated for each individual in the population.

2b. The individuals are selected according to their fitness function value.

(3) Reproduction: generate a new population of configurations from the selected one, through genetic operators (cross-over and mutation).

(4) Iteration: repeat the *Selection* and *Reproduction* until *Termination*.

(5) Termination: end if the maximum number of iterations has been reached, or the population has converged towards a particular solution.

In order to extend EDITS with genetic algorithms, we used a GA implementation available in the JGAP tool[3]. In our settings, each individual contains a sequence of boolean parameters corresponding to the activation/de-activation of the system's basic components (algorithms, cost schemes, rules, and optimizers). The configurations corresponding to such individuals constitute the populations iteratively evaluated by EDITS-GA on a given dataset.

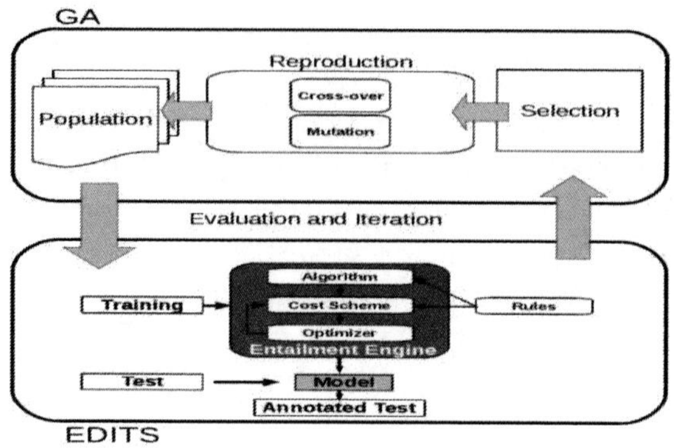

Figure 1: EDITS-GA framework.

3 Experiments

Our experiments were carried out over the datasets used in the six editions of the RTE Challenge ("Main" task data from RTE1 to RTE6). For each dataset we obtained the best model by training EDITS-GA over the development set, and evaluating the resulting model on the test pairs. To this aim, the optimization process is iterated over all the available algorithms in order to select the best combination of parameters. As *termination* criterion, we set to 20 the maximum number of iterations. To increase efficiency, we extended EDITS to pre-process each dataset using the tokenizer and stemmer available in Lucene[4]. This pre-processing phase is automatically activated when the EDITS-GA has to process non-annotated datasets. However, we also annotated the RTE corpora with the Stanford parser plugin (downloadable from the EDITS websitein order to run the syntax-based algorithms available (*e.g.* tree edit distance). The number of boolean parameters used to generate the configurations is 18. In light of this figure, it becomes evident that the number of possible configurations is too large (2^{18}=262,144) for an exhaustive training/evaluation routine over each dataset[5]. However,

[2]For instance, working on the RTE Challenge "Main" task data, the fitness function would be the *accuracy* for RTE1 to RTE5, and the *F-measure* for RTE6.

[3]http://jgap.sourceforge.net/

[4]http://lucene.apache.org/

[5]In an exploratory experiment we measured in around **4 days** the time required to train EDITS, with all possible con-

	# Systems	Best	Lowest	Average	EDITS (rank)	EDITS-GA (rank)	% Impr.	Comp. Time
RTE1	15	0.586	0.495	0.544	0.559 (8)	**0.5787** (3)	+3.52%	8m 24s
RTE2	23	0.7538	0.5288	0.5977	0.605 (6)	**0.6225** (5)	+2.89%	9m 8s
RTE3	26	0.8	0.4963	0.6237	-	**0.6875** (4)	-	9m
RTE4	26	0.746	0.516	0.5935	0.57 (17)	**0.595** (10)	+4.38%	30m 54s
RTE5	20	0.735	0.5	0.6141	0.6017 (14)	**0.6233** (9)	+3.58%	8m 23s
RTE6	18	0.4801	0.116	0.323	0.4471 (4)	**0.4673** (3)	+4.51%	1h 54m 20s

Table 1: RTE results (acc. for RTE1-RTE5, F-meas. for RTE6). For each participant, only the best run is considered.

with an average of 5 *reproductions* on each iteration, EDITS-GA makes an average of 100 configurations for each algorithm. Thanks to EDITS-GA, the average number of evaluated configurations for a single dataset is reduced to around 400[6].

Our results are summarized in Table 1, showing the total number of participating systems in each RTE Challenge, together with the highest, lowest, and average scores they achieved. Moreover, the official results obtained by EDITS are compared with the performance achieved with EDITS-GA on the same data. We can observe that, for all datasets, the results achieved by EDITS-GA significantly improve (up to 4.51%) the official EDITS results. It's also worth mentioning that such scores are always higher than the average ones obtained by participants. This confirms that EDITS-GA can be potentially used by RTE systems developers as a strong term of comparison to assess the capabilities of their own system. Since time is a crucial factor for RTE systems, it is important to remark that EDITS-GA allows to converge on a promising configuration quite efficiently. As can be seen in Table 1, the whole process takes around 9 minutes[7] for the smaller datasets (RTE1 to RTE5), and less than 2 hours for a very large dataset (RTE6). Such time analysis further proves the effectiveness of the extended EDITS-GA framework. For the sake of completeness we gave a look at the differences between the "educated guessing" done by the EDITS developers for the official RTE submissions, and the "optimal" configuration automatically selected by EDITS-GA. Surprisingly, in some cases, even a minor difference in the selected parameters leads to significant gaps in the results. For instance, in RTE6 dataset, the "guessed" configuration (Kouylekov et al., 2010) was based on the lexical overlap algorithm, setting the cost of replacing H terms without an equivalent in T to the minimal Levenshtein distance between such words and any word in T. EDITS-GA estimated, as a more promising solution, a combination of lexical overlap with a different cost scheme (based on the IDF of the terms in T). In addition, in contrast with the "guessed" configuration, stop-words filtering was selected as an option, eventually leading to a 4.51% improvement over the official RTE6 result.

figurations, over small datasets (RTE1 to RTE5).

[6]With these settings, training EDITS-GA over small datasets (RTE1 to RTE5) takes about **9 minutes** each.

[7]All time figures are calculated on an Intel(R) Xeon(R), CPU X3440 @ 2.53GHz, 8 cores with 8 GB RAM.

4 Conclusion

"Is it worth submitting this run?","How *good* is my system?". These are the typical concerns of system developers approaching the submission deadline of an RTE evaluation campaign. We addressed these issues by extending an open-source RTE system with a functionality that allows to select the most promising configuration over an annotated training set. Our contribution provides developers with a good "sparring partner" (a free and immediate term of comparison) to position the results of their approach. Experimental results prove the effectiveness of the proposed extension, showing that it allows to: *i)* achieve good performance on all the available RTE datasets, and *ii)* improve the official results, achieved with the same system, through *ad hoc* configurations manually defined by the developers team.

Acknowledgments

This work has been partially supported by the EC-funded projects CoSyne (FP7-ICT-4-24853), and Galateas (CIP-ICT PSP-2009-3-250430).

References

Margaret Aycinena, Mykel J. Kochenderfer, and David Carl Mulford. 2003. An Evolutionary Approach to Natural Language Grammar Induction. *Stanford CS 224N Natural Language Processing.*

Luisa Bentivogli, Ido Dagan, Hoa Trang Dang, Danilo Giampiccolo, Bernardo Magnini. 2009. The Fifth PASCAL Recognizing Textual Entailment Challenge. *Proceedings of the TAC 2009 Workshop.*

Ido Dagan and Oren Glickman. 2004. Probabilistic textual entailment: Generic applied modeling of language variability. *Proceedings of the PASCAL Workshop of Learning Methods for Text Understanding and Mining.*

Alejandro G. Figueroa and Günter Neumann. 2008. Genetic Algorithms for Data-driven Web Question Answering. *Evolutionary Computation 16(1) (2008) pp. 89-125.*

Andrew Hickl, John Williams, Jeremy Bensley, Kirk Roberts, Bryan Rink, and Ying Shi. 2006. Recognizing Textual Entailment with LCCs Groundhog System. *Proceedings of the Second PASCAL Challenges Workshop.*

Andrew Hickl and Jeremy Bensley. 2007. A discourse commitment-based framework for recognizing textual entailment. *Proceedings of the ACL-PASCAL Workshop on Textual Entailment and Paraphrasing.*

Houping Jia, Xiaojiang Huang, Tengfei Ma, Xiaojun Wan, and Jianguo Xiao. 2010. PKUTM Participation at TAC 2010 RTE and Summarization Track. *Proceedings of the Sixth Recognizing Textual Entailment Challenge.*

Milen Kouylekov and Matteo Negri. 2010. An Open-source Package for Recognizing Textual Entailment. *Proceedings of ACL 2010 Demo session.*

Milen Kouylekov, Yashar Mehdad, Matteo Negri, and Elena Cabrio. 2010. FBK Participation in RTE6: Main and KBP Validation Task. *Proceedings of the Sixth Recognizing Textual Entailment Challenge.*

Yashar Mehdad 2009. *Automatic Cost Estimation for Tree Edit Distance Using Particle Swarm Optimization.* Proceedings of ACL-IJCNLP 2009.

Eridan Otto and María Cristina Riff 2004. Towards an efficient evolutionary decoding algorithm for statistical machine translation. *LNAI, 2972:438447.*.

Marta Tatu and Dan Moldovan. 2007. COGEX at RTE3. *Proceedings of the ACL-PASCAL Workshop on Textual Entailment and Paraphrasing.*

Fabio Massimo Zanzotto, Marco Pennacchiotti and Alessandro Moschitti. 2007. Shallow Semantics in Fast Textual Entailment Rule Learners. *Proceedings of the Third Recognizing Textual Entailment Challenge.*

Diversity-aware Evaluation for Paraphrase Patterns

Hideki Shima
Language Technologies Institute
Carnegie Mellon University
Pittsburgh, PA, USA
hideki@cs.cmu.edu

Teruko Mitamura
Language Technologies Institute
Carnegie Mellon University
Pittsburgh, PA, USA
teruko@cs.cmu.edu

Abstract

Common evaluation metrics for paraphrase patterns do not necessarily correlate with extrinsic recognition task performance. We propose a metric which gives weight to lexical variety in paraphrase patterns; our proposed metric has a positive correlation with paraphrase recognition task performance, with a Pearson correlation of 0.5~0.7 (k=10, with "strict" judgment) in a statistically significant level (p-value<0.01).

1 Introduction

We propose a diversity-aware paraphrase evaluation metric called DIMPLE[1], which boosts the scores of lexically diverse paraphrase pairs. Paraphrase pairs or patterns are useful in various NLP related research domains, since there is a common need to automatically identify meaning equivalence between two or more texts.

Consider a paraphrase pair resource that links "killed" to "assassinated" (in the rest of this paper we denote such a rule as ⟨"killed"[2], "assassinated"[3]⟩). In automatic evaluation for Machine Translation (MT) (Zhou et al., 2006; Kauchak and Barzilay, 2006; Padó et al., 2009), this rule may enable a metric to identify phrase-level semantic similarity between a system response containing "killed", and a reference translation containing "assassinated". Similarly in query expansion for information retrieval (IR) (Riezler et al., 2007), this rule may enable a system to expand the query term "killed" with the paraphrase "assassinated", in order to match a potentially relevant document containing the expanded term.

To evaluate paraphrase patterns during pattern discovery, ideally we should use an evaluation metric that strongly predicts performance on the extrinsic task (e.g. fluency and adequacy scores in MT, mean average precision in IR) where the paraphrase patterns are used.

Many existing approaches use a paraphrase evaluation methodology where human assessors judge each paraphrase pair as to whether they have the same meaning. Over a set of paraphrase rules for one source term, Expected Precision (EP) is calculated by taking the mean of precision, or the ratio of positive labels annotated by assessors (Bannard and Callison-Burch, 2005; Callison-Burch, 2008; Kok and Brockett, 2010; Metzler et al., 2011).

The weakness of this approach is that EP is an intrinsic measure that does not necessarily predict how well a paraphrase-embedded system will perform in practice. For example, a set of paraphrase pairs ⟨"killed", "shot and killed"⟩, ⟨"killed", "reported killed"⟩ ... ⟨"killed", "killed in"⟩ may receive a perfect score of 1.0 in EP; however, these patterns do not provide lexical diversity (e.g. ⟨"killed", "assassinated"⟩) and therefore may not perform well in an application where lexical diversity is important.

The goal of this paper is to provide empirical evidence to support the assumption that the proposed paraphrase evaluation metric DIMPLE correlates better with paraphrase recognition task metric scores than previous metrics do, by rewarding lexical diverse patterns.

2 DIMPLE Metric

Patterns or rules for capturing equivalence in meaning are used in various NLP applications. In a broad sense,

[1] DIversity-aware Metric for Pattern Learning Experiments
[2] Source term/phrase that contains "killed"
[3] Paraphrase that contains "assassinated"

the terms "paraphrase" will be used to denote pairs or a set of patterns that represent semantically equivalent or close texts with different surface forms.

Given paraphrase patterns P, or the ranked list of distinct paraphrase pairs sorted by confidence in descending order, DIMPLE_k evaluates the top k patterns, and produces a real number between 0 and 1 (higher the better).

2.1 Cumulative Gain

DIMPLE is inspired by the Cumulative Gain (CG) metric (Järvelin and Kekäläinen, 2002; Kekäläinen, 2005) used in IR. CG for the top k retrieved documents is calculated as $\text{CG}_k = \sum_{i=1}^{k} gain_i$ where the gain function is human-judged relevance grade of the i-th document with respect to information need (e.g. 0 through 3 for irrelevant, marginally relevant, fairly relevant and highly relevant respectively). We take an alternative well-known formula for CG calculation, which puts stronger emphasis at higher gain: $\text{CG}_k = \sum_{i=1}^{k} (2 \wedge gain_i - 1)$.

2.2 DIMPLE Algorithm

DIMPLE is a normalized CG calculated on each paraphrase. The gain function of DIMPLE is represented as a product of pattern quality Q and lexical diversity D: $gain_i = Q_i \cdot D_i$. DIMPLE at rank k is a normalized CG_k which is defined as:

$$\text{DIMPLE}_k = \frac{\text{CG}_k}{Z} = \frac{\sum_{i=1}^{k} \{2 \wedge (Q_i \cdot D_i) - 1\}}{Z}$$

where Z is a normalization factor such that the perfect CG score is given. Since Q takes a real value between 0 and 1, and D takes an integer between 1 and 3, $Z = \sum_{i=1}^{k} \{2 \wedge 3 - 1\}$.

Being able to design Q and D independently is one of characteristics in DIMPLE. In theory, Q can be any quality measure on paraphrase patterns, such as the instance-based evaluation score (Szpektor et al., 2007), or alignment-based evaluation score (Callison-Burch et al., 2008). Similarly, D can be implemented depending on the domain task; for example, if we are interested in learning paraphrases that are out-of-vocabulary or domain-specific, D could consult a dictionary, and return a high score if the lexical entry could not be found.

The DIMPLE framework is implemented in the following way[4]. Let Q be the ratio of positive labels averaged over pairs by human assessors given p_i as to whether a paraphrase has the same meaning as the source term or not. Let D be the degree of lexical diversity of a pattern calculated using Algorithm 1 below.

Algorithm 1. D score calculation

```
Input: paraphrases {w_1, ..., w_k} for a source term s
Set history1 = extractContentWords(s)
Set history2 = stemWords(history1)
for i=1 to k do
   Set W1 = extractContentWords(w_i)
   Set W2 = stemWords(W1) // Porter stemming
   if W1==∅ || W1 ∩ history1 != ∅
      D[i] = 1 // word already seen
   else
      if W2 ∩ history2 != ∅
         D[i] = 2 // root already seen
      else
         D[i] = 3 // unseen word
      end if
      history1 = W1 ∪ history1
      history2 = W2 ∪ history2
   end if
end for
```

3 Experiment

We use the Pearson product-moment correlation coefficient to measure correlation between two vectors consisting of intrinsic and extrinsic scores on paraphrase patterns, following previous meta-evaluation research (Callison-Burch et al., 2007; Callison-Burch et al., 2008; Tratz and Hovy, 2009; Przybocki et al., 2009). By *intrinsic* score, we mean a theory-based direct assessment result on the paraphrase patterns. By *extrinsic* score, we mean to measure how much the paraphrase recognition component helps the entire system to achieve a task. The correlation score is 1 if there is a perfect positive correlation, 0 if there is no correlation and -1 if there is a perfect negative correlation.

Using a task performance score to evaluate a paraphrase generation algorithm has been studied previously (Bhagat and Ravichandran, 2008; Szpektor and Dagan, 2007; Szpektor and Dagan, 2008). A common issue in extrinsic evaluations is that it is hard to separate out errors, or contributions from other possibly complex modules. This paper presents an approach which can predict task performance in more simple experimental settings.

3.1 Annotated Paraphrase Resource

We used the paraphrase pattern dataset "paraphrase-eval" (Metzler et al., 2011; Metzler and Hovy, 2011) which contains paraphrase patterns acquired by multiple algorithms: 1) PD (Pasca and Dienes, 2005),

[4] Implementation used for this experiment is available at `http://code.google.com/p/dimple/`

which is based on the left and right n-gram contexts of the source term, with scoring based on overlap; 2) BR (Bhagat and Ravichandran, 2008), based on Noun Phrase chunks as contexts; 3) BCB (Bannard and Callison-Burch, 2005) and 4) BCB-S (Callison-Burch, 2008), which are based on monolingual phrase alignment from a bilingual corpus using a pivot. In the dataset, each paraphrase pair is assigned with an annotation as to whether a pair is a correct paraphrase or not by 2 or 3 human annotators.

The source terms are 100 verbs extracted from newswire about terrorism and American football. We selected 10 verbs according to their frequency in extrinsic task datasets (details follow in Section 3.3).

Following the methodology used in previous paraphrase evaluations (Bannard and Callison-Burch, 2005; Callison-Burch, 2008; Kok and Brockett, 2010), the labels were annotated on a pair of two sentences: an original sentence containing the source term, and the same sentence with the source term replaced with the paraphrase pattern, so that contextual information could help annotators to make consistent judgments. The judgment is based on whether the "same meaning" is present between the source term and its paraphrase. There is a lenient and a strict distinction on the "same meaning" judgments. The strict label is given when the replaced sentence is grammatically correct whereas the lenient label is given even when the sentence is grammatically incorrect.

In total, we have 10 (source terms listed in Table 1) × 4 (paraphrase generation algorithms introduced above) = 40 sets of paraphrase patterns. In each set of paraphrase patterns, there are up to 10 unique ⟨source term, paraphrase⟩ pairs.

3.2 Intrinsic Paraphrase Metrics

We will discuss the common metric EP, and its variant EPR as baselines to be compared with DIMPLE. For each metric, we used a cutoff value of k=1, 5 and 10.

EP: Our baseline is the Expected Precision at k, which is the expected number of correct paraphrases among the top k returned, and is computed as: $\mathrm{EP}_k = \frac{1}{k}\sum_{i=1}^{k} Q_i$ where Q is the ratio of positive labels. For instance, if 2 out of 3 human annotators judged that p_i = ⟨"killed", "fatally shot"⟩ has the same meaning, Q_i= 2/3.

EPR: Metzler et al., (2011) extended EP with a Redundancy judgment, which we shall call EPR where lexically redundant paraphrases did not receive a credit. Unlike Metzler et al., (2011) where humans judged redundancies, we do the judgment automatically with a Porter Stemmer (Porter, 1980) to extract and compare stemmed forms. In that way EPR's output become comparable to DIMPLE's, remaining redundancy scoring different (i.e. binary filtering in EPR and 3-level weighting in DIMPLE).

3.3 Extrinsic Evaluation Datasets

Ideally, paraphrase metric scores should correlate well with task performance metrics. To insulate the experiment from external, uncontrollable factors (e.g. errors from other task components), we created three datasets with slightly different characteristics, where the essential task of recognizing meaning equivalence between different surface texts can be conducted.

The numbers of positive-labeled pairs that we extracted for the three corpus, MSRPC, RTE and CQAE are 3900, 2805 and 27397 respectively. Table 1 shows the number of text pairs selected in which at least one of each pair contains a frequently occurring verb.

Src verb	MSRPC	RTE	CQAE
found	89	62	319
called	59	61	379
told	125	34	189
killed	48	109	277
accused	30	44	143
to take	21	23	63
reached	22	18	107
returned	14	20	57
turned	22	10	94
broke	10	10	35

Table 1. 10 most frequently occurring source verbs in three datasets. Numbers are positive-labeled pairs where the verb appears in at least one side of a pair.

MSRPC: The Microsoft Research Paraphrase Corpus (Dollan et al., 2005) contains 5800 pairs of sentences along with human annotations where positive labels mean semantic equivalence of pairs.

RTE: (Quasi-)paraphrase patterns are useful for the closely related task, Recognizing Textual Entailment. This dataset has been taken from the 2-way/3-way track at PASCAL/TAC RTE1-4. Positive examples are premise-hypothesis pairs where human annotators assigned the entailment label. The original dataset has been generated from actual applications such as Text Summarization, Information Extraction, IR, Question Answering.

CQAE: Complex Question Answering Evaluation (CQAE) dataset has been built from 6 past TREC QA tracks, i.e., "Other" QA data from TREC 2005 through 2007, relation QA data from TREC 2005 and ciQA from TREC 2006 and 2007 (Voorhees and Dang, 2005; Dang et al., 2006; Dang et al., 2007). We created unique pairs consisting of a system response (often sentence-length) and an answer nugget as positive examples, where the system response is judged by human as containing or expressing the meaning of the nugget.

3.4 Extrinsic Performance Metric

Using the dataset described in Section 3.3, performance measures for each of the 40 paraphrase sets (10 verbs times 4 generators) are calculated as the ratio of pairs correctly identified as paraphrases.

In order to make the experimental settings close to an actual system with an embedded paraphrase engine, we first apply simple unigram matching with stemming enabled. At this stage, a text with the source verb "killed" and another text with the inflectional variant "killing" would match. As an alternative approach, we consult the paraphrase pattern set trying to find a match between the texts. This identification judgment is automated, where we assume a meaning equivalence is identified between texts when the source verb matches[5] one text and one of up to 10 paraphrases in the set matches the other. Given these evaluation settings, a noisy paraphrase pair such as ⟨"killed", "to"⟩ can easily match many pairs and falsely boost the performance score. We filter such exceptional cases when the paraphrase text contains only functional words.

3.5 Results

We conducted experiments to provide evidence that the Pearson correlation coefficient of DIMPLE is higher than that of the other two baselines. Table 2 and 3 below present the result where each number is the correlation calculated on the 40 data points.

	EP_k			EPR_k			$DIMPLE_k$		
	k=1	5	10	1	5	10	1	5	10
MSRPC	-0.02	-0.24	-0.11	0.33	0.27	-0.12	0.32	0.20	0.25
RTE	0.13	-0.05	0.11	0.33	0.12	0.09	**0.46**	0.25	0.37
CQAE	0.08	-0.09	0.00	-0.02	-0.08	-0.13	0.35	0.25	**0.40**

Table 2. Correlation between intrinsic paraphrase metrics and extrinsic paraphrase recognition task metrics where DIMPLE's Q score is based on *lenient* judgment. Bold figures indicate statistical significance of the correlation statistics (null-hypothesis tested: "there is no correlation", p-value<0.01).

	EP_k			EPR_k			$DIMPLE_k$		
	k=1	5	10	1	5	10	1	5	10
MSRPC	0.12	0.13	0.19	0.26	0.36	0.37	0.26	0.35	**0.52**
RTE	0.34	0.34	0.29	**0.43**	**0.41**	**0.38**	**0.49**	**0.55**	**0.58**
CQAE	**0.44**	**0.51**	**0.47**	0.37	**0.60**	**0.55**	0.37	**0.70**	**0.70**

Table 3. Same as the Table 2, except that the Q score is based on *strict* judgment.

Table 2 shows that correlations are almost always close to 0, indicating that EP does not correlate with the extrinsic measures when the Q score is calculated in lenient judgment mode. On the other hand, when the Q function is based on strict judgments, EP scores sometimes show a medium positive correlation with the extrinsic task performance, such as on the CQAE dataset.

In both tables, there is a general trend where the correlation scores fall in the same relative order (given the same cut-off value): EP < EPR < DIMPLE. This suggests that DIMPLE has a higher correlation than the other two baselines, given the task performance measure we experimented with. As we can see from Table 2, DIMPLE correlates well with paraphrase task performance, especially when the cutoff value k is 5 or 10. The higher values in Table 3 (compared to Table 2) show that the strict judgment used for intrinsic metric calculation is preferable over the lenient one.

4 Conclusion and Future Works

We proposed a novel paraphrase evaluation metric called DIMPLE, which gives weight to lexical variety. We built large scale datasets from three sources and conducted extrinsic evaluations where paraphrase recognition is involved. Experimental results showed that Pearson correlation statistics for DIMPLE are approximately 0.5 to 0.7 (when k=10 and "strict" annotations are used to calculate the score), which is higher than scores for the commonly used EP and EPR metrics.

Future works include applying DIMPLE on patterns for other tasks where lexical diversity matters (e.g. Relation Extraction) with a customized Q and D functions. If Q function can be also calculated fully automatically, DIMPLE may be useful for learning lexically diverse pattern learning when it is incorporated into optimization criteria.

Acknowledgments

We gratefully acknowledges the support of Defense Advanced Research Projects Agency (DARPA) Machine Reading Program under Air Force Research Laboratory (AFRL) prime contract no. FA8750-09-C-0172. Any opinions, findings, and conclusion or recommendations expressed in this material are those of the author(s) and do not necessarily reflect the view of the DARPA, AFRL, or the US government. We also thank Donald Metzler et al. for sharing their data, and Eric Nyberg and anonymous reviewers for their helpful comments.

[5] We consider word boundaries when matching texts, e.g. "skilled" and "killed" do not match.

References

Bannard, Colin and Chris Callison-Burch. 2005. Paraphrasing with Bilingual Parallel Corpora. In Proceedings of ACL 2005.

Bhagat, Rahul, Patrick Pantel, Eduard Hovy, and Marina Rey. 2007. LEDIR: An Unsupervised Algorithm for Learning Directionality of Inference Rules. In Proceedings of EMNLP-CoNLL 2007.

Bhagat, Rahul and Deepak Ravichandran. 2008. Large Scale Acquisition of Paraphrases for Learning Surface Patterns. In Proceedings of ACL-08: HLT.

Callison-Burch, Chris. 2008. Syntactic Constraints on Paraphrases Extracted from Parallel Corpora. In Proceedings of EMNLP 2008.

Callison-Burch, Chris, Cameron Fordyce, Philipp Koehn, Christof Monz, and Josh Schroeder. 2007. (Meta-) Evaluation of Machine Translation. In Proceedings of the Second Workshop on Statistical Machine Translation - StatMT '07.

Callison-Burch, Chris, Cameron Fordyce, Philipp Koehn, Christof Monz, and Josh Schroeder. 2008. Further Meta-Evaluation of Machine Translation. In Proceedings of the Third Workshop on Statistical Machine Translation - StatMT '08.

Dang, Hoa Trang, Jimmy Lin, and Diane Kelly. 2006. Overview of the TREC 2006 Question Answering Track. In Proceedings of TREC 2006.

Dang, Hoa Trang, Diane Kelly, and Jimmy Lin. 2007. Overview of the TREC 2007 Question Answering Track. In Proceedings of TREC 2007.

Dolan, William B., and Chris Brockett. 2005. Automatically Constructing a Corpus of Sentential Paraphrases. In Proceedings of the Third International Workshop on Paraphrasing (IWP2005).

Järvelin, Kalervo, Jaana Kekäläinen. 2002. Cumulated Gain-based Evaluation of IR Techniques. ACM Trans. Inf. Syst., Vol. 20, No. 4. (October 2002), pp. 422-446.

Kauchak, David, and Regina Barzilay. 2006. Paraphrasing for Automatic Evaluation. In Proceedings of HLT-NAACL 2006.

Kekäläinen, Jaana. 2005. Binary and Graded Relevance in IR Evaluations – Comparison of the Effects on Ranking of IR Systems. Information Processing & Management, 41, 1019-1033.

Kok, Stanley and Chris Brockett. 2010. Hitting the Right Paraphrases in Good Time. In Proceedings of HLT-NAACL 2010.

Lin, Dekang, and Patrick Pantel. 2001. DIRT - Discovery of Inference Rules from Text. In Proceedings of the seventh ACM SIGKDD international conference on Knowledge discovery and data mining - KDD '01 323-328.

Metzler, Donald, Eduard Hovy, and Chunliang Zhang. 2011. An Empirical Evaluation of Data-Driven Paraphrase Generation Techniques. In Proceedings of ACL-HLT 2011.

Metzler, Donald and Eduard Hovy. 2011. Mavuno: A Scalable and Effective Hadoop-Based Paraphrase Harvesting System. To appear in Proceedings of the KDD Workshop on Large-scale Data Mining: Theory and Applications (LDMTA 2011).

Miller, Geroge A. 1995. Wordnet: A Lexical Database for English. CACM, 38(11):39-41.

Padó, Sebastian, Michel Galley, Dan Jurafsky, and Christopher D. Manning. 2009. Robust Machine Translation Evaluation with Entailment Features. In Proceedings of ACL-IJCNLP '09.

Pasca, Marius and Pter Dienes. 2005. Aligning Needles in a Haystack: Paraphrase Acquisition Across the Web. In Processing of IJCNLP 2005.

Porter, Martin F. 1980. An Algorithm for Suffix Stripping, Program, 14(3): 130–137.

Przybocki, Mark, Kay Peterson, Sébastien Bronsart, and Gregory Sanders. 2009. The NIST 2008 Metrics for Machine Translation Challenge—Overview, Methodology, Metrics, and Results. Machine Translation, Volume 23 Issue 2-3.

Riezler, Stefan, Alexander Vasserman, Ioannis Tsochantaridis, Vibhu Mittal, and Yi Liu. 2007. Statistical Machine Translation for Query Expansion in Answer Retrieval. In Proceedings of ACL 2007.

Szpektor, Idan and Ido Dagan. 2007. Learning Canonical Forms of Entailment Rules. In Proceedings of RANLP 2007.

Szpektor, Idan, Eyal Shnarch and Ido Dagan. 2007. Instance-based Evaluation of Entailment Rule Acquisition. In Proceedings of ACL 2007.

Szpektor, Idan and Ido Dagan. 2008. Learning Entailment Rules for Unary Templates. In Proceedings of COLING 2008.

Tratz, Stephen and Eduard Hovy. 2009. BEwT-E for TAC 2009's AESOP Task. In Proceedings of TAC-09. Gaithersburg, Maryland.

Voorhees, Ellen M., and Hoa Trang Dang. 2005. Overview of the TREC 2005 Question Answering Track. In Proceedings of TREC 2005.

Zhou, Liang, Chin-Yew Lin, and Eduard Hovy. 2006. Re-evaluating Machine Translation Results with Paraphrase Support. In Proceedings of EMNLP 2006.

Representing and resolving ambiguities in ontology-based question answering

Christina Unger **Philipp Cimiano**
Cognitive Interaction Technology – Center of Excellence (CITEC),
Universität Bielefeld, Germany
{cunger|cimiano}@cit-ec.uni-bielefeld.de

Abstract

Ambiguities are ubiquitous in natural language and pose a major challenge for the automatic interpretation of natural language expressions. In this paper we focus on different types of lexical ambiguities that play a role in the context of ontology-based question answering, and explore strategies for capturing and resolving them. We show that by employing underspecification techniques and by using ontological reasoning in order to filter out inconsistent interpretations as early as possible, the overall number of interpretations can be effectively reduced by 44 %.

1 Introduction

Ambiguities are ubiquitous in natural language. They pose a key challenge for the automatic interpretation of natural language expressions and have been recognized as a central issue in question answering (e.g. in (Burger et al., 2001)). In general, ambiguities comprise all cases in which natural language expressions (simple or complex) can have more than one meaning. These cases roughly fall into two classes: They either concern *structural* properties of an expression, e.g. different parses due to alternative preposition or modifier attachments and different quantifier scopings, or they concern alternative meanings of *lexical* items. It is these latter ambiguities, ambiguities with respect to lexical meaning, that we are interested in. More specifically, we will look at ambiguities in the context of ontology-based interpretation of natural language.

The meaning of a natural language expression in the context of ontology-based interpretation is the ontology concept that this expression verbalizes. For example, the expression *city* can refer to a class `geo:city` (where `geo` is the namespace of the corresponding ontology), and the expression *inhabitants* can refer to a property `geo:population`. The correspondence between natural language expressions and ontology concepts need not be one-to-one. On the one hand side, different natural language expressions can refer to a single ontology concept, e.g. *flows through*, *crosses through* and *traverses* could be three ways of expressing an ontological property `geo:flowsThrough`. On the other hand, one natural language expression can refer to different ontology concepts. For example, the verb *has* is vague with respect to the relation it expresses – it could map to `geo:flowsThrough` (in the case of rivers) as well as `geo:inState` (in the case of cities). Such mismatches between the linguistic meaning of an expression, i.e. the user's conceptual model, and the conceptual model in the ontology give rise to a number of ambiguities. We will give a detailed overview of those ambiguities in Section 3, after introducing preliminaries in Section 2.

For a question answering system, there are mainly two ways to resolve ambiguities: by interactive clarification and by means of background knowledge and the context with respect to which a question is asked and answered. The former is, for example, pursued by the question answering system FREyA (Damljanovic et al., 2010). The latter is incorporated in some recent work in machine learning. For example, (Kate & Mooney, 2007) investigate the task of learning a semantic parser from a corpus whith sentences annotated with multiple, alternative interpretations, and (Zettlemoyer & Collins, 2009) explore an unsupervised algorithm for learning mappings from natural language sentences to logical forms, with context accounted for by hidden variables in a perceptron.

In ontology-based question answering, context as well as domain knowledge is provided by the ontology. In this paper we explore how a given ontology can be exploited for ambiguity resolution. We will consider two strategies in Section 4. The first one consists in simply enumerating all possible interpretations. Since this is not efficient (and maybe not even feasible), we will use underspecification techniques for representing ambiguities in a much more compact way and then present a strategy for resolving ambiguities by means of ontological reasoning, so that the number of interpretations that have to be considered in the end is relatively small and does not comprise inconsistent and therefore undesired interpretations. We will summarize with quantitative results in Section 5.

2 Preliminaries

All examples throughout the paper will be based on Raymond Mooney's *GeoBase*[1] dataset and the DBpedia question set published in the context of the *1st Workshop on Question Answering Over Linked Data* (QALD-1)[2]. The former is a relatively small and well-organized domain, while the latter is considerably larger and much more heterogenous. It is interesting to note that ontological ambiguituies turn out to be very wide-spread even in a small and homogenuous domain like GeoBase (see Section 3 for specific results).

For specifying entries of a grammar that a question answering system might work with, we will use the general and principled linguistic representations that our question answering system *Pythia*[3] (Unger et al., 2010) relies on, as they are suitable for dealing with a wide range of natural language phenomena. Syntactic representations will be trees from *Lexicalized Tree Adjoining Grammar* (LTAG (Schabes, 1990)). The syntactic representation of a lexical item is a tree constituting an extended projection of that item, spanning all of its syntactic and semantic arguments. Argument slots are nodes marked with a down arrow (↓), for which trees with the same root category can be substituted. For example, the tree for a transitive verb like *borders* looks as follows:

1.

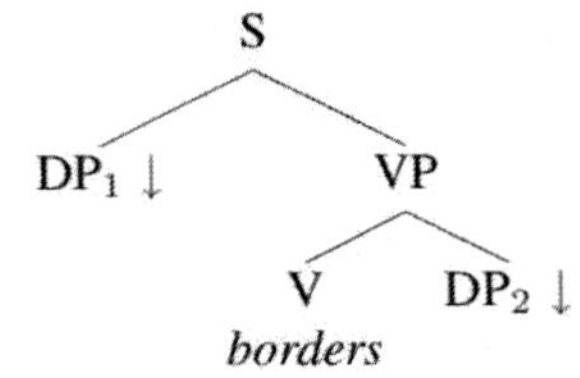

The domain of the verb thus spans a whole sentence, containing its two nominal arguments – one in subject position and one in object position. The corresponding nodes, DP_1 and DP_2, are slots for which any DP-tree can be substituted. For example, substituting the two trees in 2 for subject and object DP, respectively, yields the tree in 3.

2. (a)

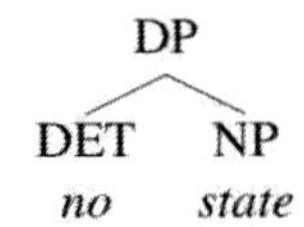

(b)

3.

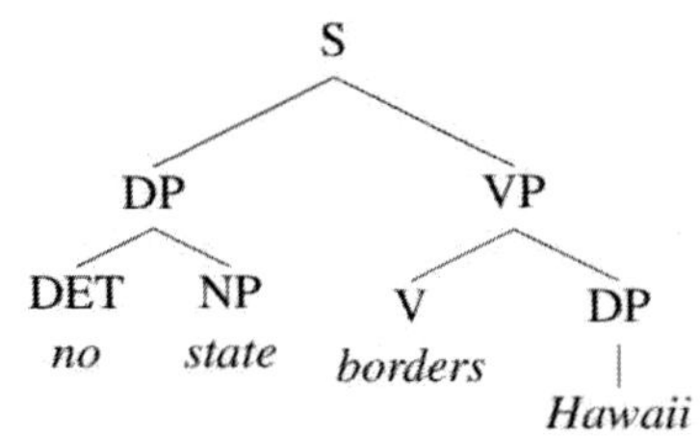

As semantic representations we take DUDEs (Cimiano, 2009), representations similar to structures from *Underspecified Discourse Representation Theory* (UDRT (Reyle, 1993)), extended with some additional information that allows for flexible meaning composition in parallel to the construction of LTAG trees. The DUDE for the verb *to border*, for example, would be the following (in a slightly simplified version):

geo:borders (x, y)
$(DP_1, x), (DP_2, y)$

[1] cs.utexas.edu/users/ml/nldata/geoquery.html
[2] http://www.sc.cit-ec.uni-bielefeld.de/qald-1
[3] http://www.sc.cit-ec.uni-bielefeld.de/pythia

It provides the predicate geo:borders corresponding to the intended concept in the ontology. This correspondence is ensured by using the vocabulary of the ontology, i.e. by using the URI[4] of the concept instead of a more generic predicate. The prefix geo specifies the namespace, in this case the one of the GeoBase ontology. Furthermore, the semantic representation contains information about which substitution nodes in the syntactic structure provide the semantic arguments x and y. That is, the semantic referent provided by the meaning of the tree substituted for DP_1 corresponds to the first argument x of the semantic predicate, while the semantic referent provided by the meaning of the tree substituted for DP_2 corresponds to the second argument y. The uppermost row of the box contains the referent that is introduced by the expression. For example, the DUDE for *Hawaii* (paired with the tree in 2b) would be the following:

h
geo:name (h, 'hawaii')

It introduces a referent h which is related to the literal 'hawaii' by means of the relation geo:name. As it does not have any arguments, the third row is empty. The bottom-most row, empty in both DUDEs, is for selectional restrictions of predicates; we will see those in Section 4.

Parallel to substituting the DP-tree in 2b for the DP_1-slot in 1, the DUDE for *Hawaii* is combined with the DUDE for *borders*, amounting to the saturation of the argument (DP_2, y) by unifying the variables h and y, yielding the following DUDE:

h
geo:borders (x, h) geo:name (h, 'hawaii')
(DP_1, x)

Substituting the subject argument *no state* involves quantifier representations which we will gloss over as they do not play a role in this paper. At this point it suffices to say that we implement the treatment of quantifier scope in UDRT without modifications.

Once a meaning representation for a question is built, it is translated into a SPARQL query, which can then be evaluated with respect to a given dataset.

Not a lot hinges on the exact choice of the formalisms; we could as well have chosen any other syntactic and semantic formalism that allows the incorporation of underspecification mechanisms. The same holds for the use of SPARQL as formal query language. The reason for choosing SPARQL is that it is the standard query language for the Semantic Web[5]; we therefore feel safe in relying on the reader's familiarity with SPARQL and use SPARQL queries without further explanation.

3 Types of ambiguities

As described in the introduction above, a central task in ontology-based interpretation is the mapping of a natural language expression to an ontology concept. And this mapping gives rise to several different cases of ambiguities.

First, ambiguities can arise due to homonymy of a natural language expression, i.e. an expression that has several lexical meanings, where each of these meanings can be mapped to one ontology concept unambiguously. The ambiguity is inherent to the expression and is independent of any domain or ontology. This is what in linguistic contexts is called a lexical ambiguity. A classical example is the noun *bank*, which can mean a financial institution, a kind of seating, the edge of a river, and a range of other disjoint, non-overlapping alternatives. An example in the geographical domain is *New York*. It can mean either New York city, in this case it would be mapped to the ontological entity geo:new_york_city, or New York state, in this case it would be mapped to the entity geo:new_york. Ambiguous names are actually the only case of such ambiguities that occur in the GeoBase dataset.

Another kind of ambiguities is due to mismatches between a user's concept of the meaning of an expression and the modelling of this meaning in the ontology. For example, if the ontology modelling is more fine-grained than the meaning

[4]URI stands for *Uniform Resource Identifier*. URIs uniquely identify resources on the Web. For an overview, see, e.g., http://www.w3.org/Addressing/.

[5]For the W3C reference, see http://www.w3.org/TR/rdf-sparql-query/.

of a natural language expression, then an expression with one meaning can be mapped to several ontology concepts. These concepts could differ extensionally as well as intensionally. An example is the above mentioned expression *starring*, that an ontology engineer could want to comprise only leading roles or also include supporting roles. If he decides to model this distinction and introduces two properties, then the ontological model is more fine-grained than the meaning of the natural language expression, which could be seen as corresponding to the union of both ontology properties. Another example is the expression *inhabitants* in question 4, which can be mapped either to `<http://dbpedia.org/property/population>` or to `<http://dbpedia.org/ontology/populationUrban>`. For most cities, both alternatives give a result, but they differ slightly, as one captures only the core urban area while the other also includes the outskirts. For some city, even only one of them might be specified in the dataset.

4. *Which cities have more than two million inhabitants?*

Such ambiguities occur in larger datasets like DBpedia with a wide range of common nouns and transitive verbs. In the QALD-1 training questions for DBpedia, for example, at least 16 % of the questions contain expressions that do not have a unique ontological correspondent.

Another source for ambiguities is the large number of vague and context-dependent expressions in natural language. While it is not possible to pinpoint such expressions to a fully specified lexical meaning, a question answering system needs to map them to one (or more) specific concept(s) in the ontology. Often there are several mapping possibilities, sometimes depending on the linguistic context of the expression.

An example for context-dependent expressions in the geographical domain is the adjective *big*: it refers to size (of a city or a state) either with respect to population or with respect to area. For the question 5a, for example, two queries could be intended – one refering to population and one refering to area. They are given in 5b and 5c.

5. (a) *What is the biggest city?*

   (b)
```
SELECT ?s WHERE {
  ?s a geo:city .
  ?s geo:population ?p . }
ORDER BY DESC ?p LIMIT 1
```

   (c)
```
SELECT ?s WHERE {
  ?s a geo:city .
  ?s geo:area ?a . }
ORDER BY DESC ?a LIMIT 1
```

Without further clarification – either by means of a clarification dialog with the user (e.g. employed by FREyA (Damljanovic et al., 2010)) or an explicit disambiguation as in *What is the biggest city by area?* – both interpretations are possible and adequate. That is, the adjective *big* introduces two mapping alternatives that both lead to a consistent interpretation.

A slightly different example are vague expressions. Consider the questions 6a and 7a. The verb *has* refers either to the object property `flowsThrough`, when relating states and rivers, or to the object property `inState`, when relating states and cities. The corresponding queries are given in 6b and 7b.

6. (a) *Which state has the most rivers?*

   (b)
```
SELECT COUNT(?s) AS ?n WHERE {
  ?s a geo:state .
  ?r a geo:river .
  ?r geo:flowsThrough ?s. }
ORDER BY DESC ?n LIMIT 1
```

7. (a) *Which state has the most cities?*

   (b)
```
SELECT COUNT(?s) AS ?n WHERE {
  ?s a geo:state .
  ?c a geo:city .
  ?c geo:inState ?s. }
ORDER BY DESC ?n LIMIT 1
```

In contrast to the example of *big* above, these two interpretations, `flowsThrough` and `inState`, are exclusive alternatives: only one of them is admissible, depending on the linguistic context. This is due to the sortal restrictions of those properties: `flowsThrough` only allows rivers as domain, whereas `inState` only allows cities as domain.

This kind of ambiguities are very frequent, as a lot of user questions contain semantically light expressions, e.g. the copula verb *be*, the verb *have*, and prepositions like *of*, *in* and *with* (cf. (Cimiano & Minock, 2009)) – expressions which are vague and do not specify the exact relation they are denoting. In the 880 user questions that Mooney provides, there are 1278 occurences of the light expressions *is/are*, *has/have*, *with*, *in*, and *of*, in addition to 151 ocurrences of the context-dependent expressions *big*, *small*, and *major*.

4 Capturing and resolving ambiguities

When constructing a semantic representation and a formal query, all possible alternative meanings have to be considered. We will look at two strategies to do so: simply enumerating all interpretations (constructing a different semantic representation and query for every possible interpretation), and underspecification (constructing only one underspecified representation that subsumes all different interpretations).

4.1 Enumeration

Consider the example of a lexically ambiguous question in 8a. It contains two ambiguous expressions: *New York* can refer either to the city or the state, and *big* can refer to size either with respect to area or with respect to population. This leads to four possible interpretations of the questions, given in 8b–8e.

8. (a) *How big is New York?*
   (b) `SELECT ?a WHERE {`
       `geo:new_york_city geo:area ?a . }`
   (c) `SELECT ?p WHERE {`
       `geo:new_york_city geo:population ?p.}`
   (d) `SELECT ?a WHERE {`
       `geo:new_york geo:area ?a . }`
   (e) `SELECT ?p WHERE {`
       `geo:new_york geo:population ?p . }`

Since the question in 8a can indeed have all four interpretations, all of them should be captured. The enumeration strategy amounts to constructing all four queries. In order to do so, we specify two lexical entries for *New York* and two lexical entries for the adjective *big* – one for each reading. For *big*, these two entries are given in 9 and 10. The syntactic tree is the same for both, while the semantic representations differ: one refers to the property `geo:area` and one refers to the property `geo:population`.

9.
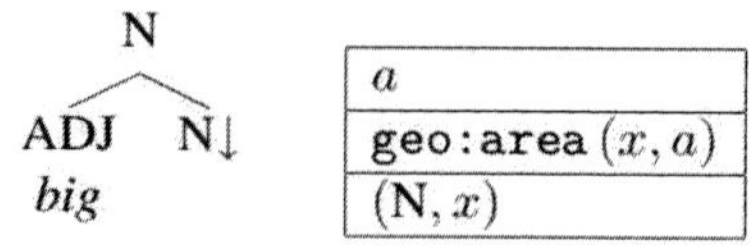

10.
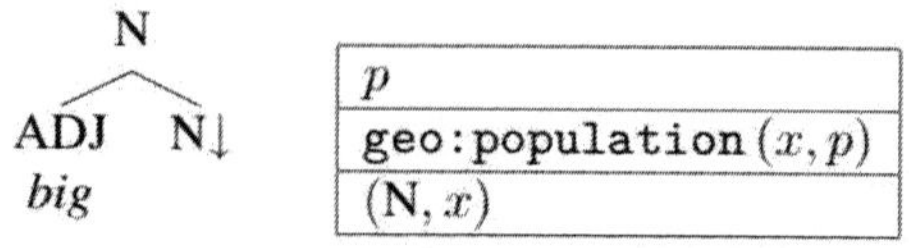

When parsing the question *How big is New York*, both entries for *big* are found during lexical lookup, and analogously two entries for *New York* are found. The interpretation process will use all of them and therefore construct four queries, 8b–8e.

Vague and context-dependent expressions can be treated similarly. The verb *to have*, for example, can map either to the property `flowsThrough`, in the case of rivers, or to the property `inState`, in the case of cities. Now we could simply specify two lexical entries *to have* – one using the meaning `flowsThrough` and one using the meaning `inState`. However, contrary to lexical ambiguities, these are not real alternatives in the sense that both lead to consistent readings. The former is only possible if the relevant argument is a river, the latter is only relevant if the relevant argument is a city. So in order not to derive inconsistent interpretations, we need to capture the sortal restrictions attached to such exclusive alternatives. This will be discussed in the next section.

4.2 Adding sortal restrictions

A straightforward way to capture ambiguities consists in enumerating all possible interpretations and thus in constructing all corresponding formal queries. We did this by specifying a separate lexical entry for every interpretation. The only difficulty that arises is that we have to capture the sortal restrictions that come with some natural language expressions. In order to do so, we add sortal restrictions to our semantic representation format.

Sortal restrictions will be of the general form *variable*^`class`. For example, the sortal restriction that instances of the variable x must belong to the class `river` in our domain would be represented as x^`geo:river`. Such sortal restrictions are added as a list to our DUDEs. For example, for the verb *has* we specify two lexical entries. One maps *has* to the property `flowThrough`, specifying the sortal restriction that the first argument of this property must belong to the class `river`. This entry looks as follows:

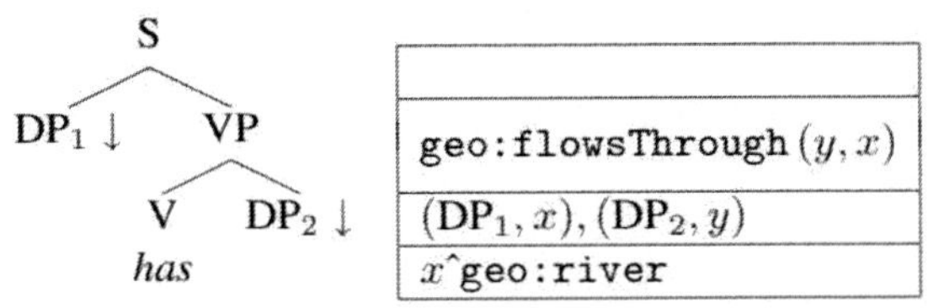

The other lexical entry for *has* consists of the same syntactic tree and a semantic representation that maps *has* to the property `inState` and contains the restriction that the first argument of this property must belong to the class `city`. It looks as follows:

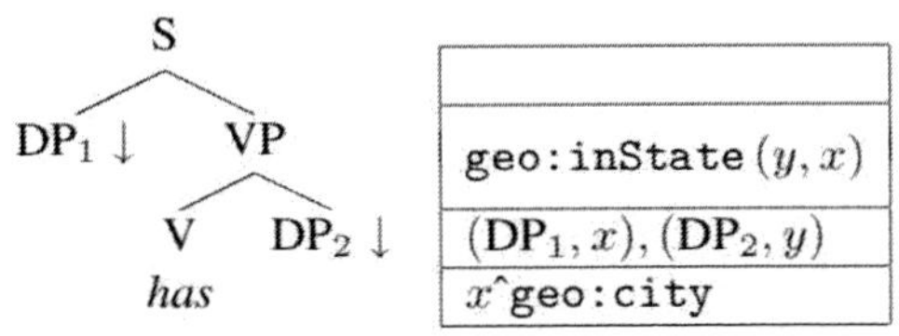

When a question containg the verb *has*, like 11a, is parsed, both interpretations for *has* are found during lexical lookup and two semantic representations are constructed, both containing a sortal restriction. When translating the semantic representations into a formal query, the sortal restriction is simply added as a condition. For 11a, the two corresponding queries are given in 11b (mapping *has* to `flowsThrough`) and 11c (mapping *has* `inState`). The contribution of the sortal restriction is boxed.

11. (a) *Which state has the most rivers?*

(b)
```
SELECT COUNT(?r) as ?c WHERE {
?s a geo:state .
?r a geo:river .
?r geo:flowsThrough ?s .
?r a geo:river . }
ORDER BY ?c DESC LIMIT 1
```

(c)
```
SELECT COUNT(?r) as ?c WHERE {
?s a geo:state .
?r a geo:river .
?r geo:inState ?s .
?r a geo:city . }
ORDER BY ?c DESC LIMIT 1
```

In the first case, 11b, the sortal restriction adds a redundant condition and will have no effect. We can say that the sortal restriction is satisfied. In the second case, in 11c, however, the sortal restriction adds a condition that is inconsistent with the other conditions, assuming that the classes `river` and `city` are properly specified as disjoint. The query will therefore not yield any results, as no instantiiation of `r` can be found that belongs to both classes. That is, in the context of rivers only the interpretation using `flowsThrough` leads to results.

Actually, the sortal restriction in 11c is already implicitly specified in the ontological relation `inState`: there is no river that is related to a state with this property. However, this is not necessarily the case and there are indeed queries where the sortal restriction has to be included explicitly. One example is the interpretation of the adjective *major* in noun phrases like *major city* and *major state*. Although with respect to the geographical domain *major* always expresses the property of having a population greater than a certain threshold, this threshold differs for cities and states: *major* with respect to cities is interpreted as having a population greater than, say, 150 000, while *major* with respect to states is interpreted as having a population greater than, say, 10 000 000. Treating *major* as ambiguous between those two readings without specifying a sortal restriction would lead to two readings for the noun phrase *major city*, sketched in 12. Both would yield non-empty results and there is no way to tell which one is the correct one.

12. (a)
```
SELECT ?c WHERE {
?c a geo:city .
?c geo:population ?p .
FILTER ( ?p > 150000 ) }
```

(b)
```
SELECT ?c WHERE {
?c a geo:city .
?c geo:population ?p .
FILTER ( ?p > 10000000 ) }
```

Specifying sortal restrictions, on the other hand, would add the boxed material in 13, thereby causing the wrong reading in 13b to return no results.

13. (a)
```
SELECT ?c WHERE {
?c a geo:city .
?c geo:population ?p .
```

```
    FILTER ( ?p > 150000 ) .
    ?c a geo:city .  }
(b) SELECT ?c WHERE {
    ?c a geo:city .
    ?c geo:population ?p .
    FILTER ( ?p > 10000000 ) .
    ?c a geo:state .  }
```

The enumeration strategy thus relies on a conflict that results in queries which return no result. Unwanted interpretations are thereby filtered out automatically. But two problems arise here. The first one is that we have no way to distinguish between queries that return no result due to an inconsistency introduced by a sortal restriction, and queries that return no result, because there is none, as in the case of *Which states border Hawaii?*. The second problem concerns the number of readings that are constructed. In view of the large number of ambiguities, even in the restricted geographical domain we used, user questions easily lead to 20 or 30 different possible interpretations. In cases in which several natural language terms can be mapped to many different ontological concepts, this number rises. Enumerating all alternative interpretations is therefore not efficient. A more practical alternative is to construct one underspecified representation instead and then infer a specific interpretation in a given context. We will explore this strategy in the next section.

4.3 Underspecification

In the following, we will explore a strategy for representing and resolving ambiguities that uses underspecification and ontological reasoning in order to keep the number of constructed interpretations to a minimum. For a general overview of underspecification formalisms and their applicability to linguistic phenomena see (Bunt, 2007).

In order not to construct a different query for every interpretation, we do not any longer specify separate lexical entries for each mapping but rather combine them by using an underspecified semantic representation. In the case of *has*, for example, we do not specify two lexical entries – one with a semantic representation using `flowsThrough` and one entry with a representation using `inState` – but instead specify only one lexical entry with a representation using a metavariable, and additionally specify which properties this metavariable stands for under which conditions.

So first we extend DUDEs such that they now can contain metavariables, and instead of a list of sortal restrictions contain a list of *metavariable specifications*, i.e. possible instantiations of a metavariable given that certain sortal restrictions are satisfied, where sortal restrictions can concern any of the property's arguments. Metavariable specifications take the following general form:

$$\begin{aligned}\mathcal{P} \rightarrow\ & \mathtt{p}_1\ (x = \mathtt{class}_1, \ldots, y = \mathtt{class}_2)\\ \mid\ & \mathtt{p}_2\ (x = \mathtt{class}_3, \ldots, y = \mathtt{class}_4)\\ \mid\ & \ldots\\ \mid\ & \mathtt{p}_n\ (x = \mathtt{class}_i, \ldots, y = \mathtt{class}_j)\end{aligned}$$

This expresses that some metavariable $\mathcal{P}$ stands for a property $\mathtt{p}_1$ if the types of the arguments $x, \ldots, y$ are equal to or a subset of $\mathtt{class}_1$,...,$\mathtt{class}_2$, and stands for some other property if the types of the arguments correspond to some other classes. For example, as interpretation of *has*, we would chose a metavariable $\mathcal{P}$ with a specification stating that $\mathcal{P}$ stands for the property `flowsThrough` if the first argument belongs to class `river`, and stands for the property `inState` if the first argument belongs to the class `city`. Thus, the lexical entry for *has* would contain the following underspecified semantic representation.

14. *Lexical meaning of 'has':*

$\mathcal{P}\ (y, x)$
$(\mathrm{DP}_1, x), (\mathrm{DP}_2, y)$
$\mathcal{P} \rightarrow$ `geo:flowsThrough` $(y =$ `geo:river`$)$ $\mid$ `geo:inState` $(y =$ `geo:city`$)$

Now this underspecified semantic representation has to be specified in order to lead to a SPARQL query that can be evaluated w.r.t. the knowledge base. That means, in the course of interpretation we need to determine which class an instantiation of y belongs to and accordingly substitute $\mathcal{P}$ by the property `flowsThrough` or `inState`. In the following section, we sketch a way of exploiting the ontology to this end.

4.4 Reducing alternatives with ontological reasoning

In order to filter out interpretations that are inconsistent as early as possible and thereby reduce the number of interpretations during the course of a derivation, we check whether the type information of a variable that is unified is consistent with the sortal restrictions connected to the metavariables. This check is performed at every relevant step in a derivation, so that inconsistent readings are not allowed to percolate and multiply. Let us demonstrate this strategy by means of the example *Which state has the biggest city?*.

In order to build the noun phrase *the biggest city*, the meaning representation of the superlative *biggest*, given in 15, is combined with that of the noun *city*, which simply contributes the predication geo:city (y), by means of unification.

15.

z
$\mathcal{Q}\,(y,z)$
(N, y)
$\mathcal{Q} \to$ geo:area($y =$ geo:city $\sqcup$ geo:state) | geo:population($y =$ geo:city $\sqcup$ geo:state)

The exact details of combining meaning representations do not matter here. What we want to focus on is the metavariable $\mathcal{Q}$ that *biggest* introduces. When combining 15 with the meaning of *city*, we can check whether the type information connected to the unified referent y is compatible with the domain restrictions of $\mathcal{Q}'s$ interpretations. One way to do this is by integrating an OWL reasoner and checking the satisfiability of

geo:city $\sqcap$ (geo:city $\sqcup$ geo:state)

(for both interpretations of $\mathcal{Q}$, as the restrictions on y are the same). Since this is indeed satisfiable, both interpretations are possible, thus cannot be discarded, and the resulting meaning representation of *the biggest city* is the following:

$y\ z$
geo:city(y) $\mathcal{Q}\,(y,z)$ $max(z)$
$\mathcal{Q} \to$ geo:area($y =$ geo:city $\sqcup$ geo:state) | geo:population($y =$ geo:city $\sqcup$ geo:state)

This is desired, as the ambiguity of *biggest* is a lexical ambiguity that could only be resolved by the user specifying which reading s/he intended.

In a next step, the above representation is combined with the semantic representation of the verb *has*, given in 14. Now the type information of the unified variable y has to be checked for compatibility with instantiations of an additional metavariable, $\mathcal{P}$. The OWL reasoner would therefore have to check the satisfiability of the following two expressions:

16. (a) geo:city $\sqcap$ geo:river
    (b) geo:city $\sqcap$ geo:city

While 16b succeeds trivially, 16a fails, assuming that the two classes geo:river and geo:city are specified as disjoint in the ontology. Therefore the instantiation of $\mathcal{P}$ as geo:flowsThrough is not consistent and can be discarded, leading to the following combined meaning representation, where $\mathcal{P}$ is replaced by its only remaining instantiation geo:inState:

$y\ z$
geo:city(y)   geo:inState (y,x) $\mathcal{Q}\,(y,z)$
(DP_1, x)
$\mathcal{Q} \to$ geo:area($y =$ geo:city $\sqcup$ geo:state) | geo:population($y =$ geo:city $\sqcup$ geo:state)

Finally, this meaning representation is combined with the meaning representation of *which state*, which simply contributes the predication geo:state (x). As the unified variable x does not occur in any metavariable specification, nothing further needs to be checked. The final meaning representation thus leaves one metavariable with two possible instantiations and will lead to the following two corresponding SPARQL queries:

17. (a)
```
SELECT ?x WHERE {
?x a geo:city .
?y a geo:state.
?x geo:population ?z .
?x geo:inState ?y . }
ORDER BY DESC(?z) LIMIT 1
```
(b)
```
SELECT ?x WHERE {
?x a geo:city .
?y a geo:state.
?x geo:area ?z .
?x geo:inState ?y . }
ORDER BY DESC(?z) LIMIT 1
```

Note that if the ambiguity of the metavariable $\mathcal{P}$ were not resolved, we would have ended up with four SPARQL queries, where two of them use the relation `geo:flowsThrough` and therefore yield empty results. So in this case, we reduced the number of constructed queries by half by discarding inconsistent readings. We therefore solved the problems mentioned at the end of 4.2: The number of constructed queries is reduced, and since we discard inconsistent readings, null answers can only be due to the lack of data in the knowledge base but not cannot anymore be due to inconsistencies in the generated queries.

5 Implementation and results

In order to see that the possibility of reducing the number of interpretations during a derivation does not only exist in a small number of cases, we applied Pythia to Mooney's 880 user questions, implementing the underspecification strategy in 4.3 and the reduction strategy in 4.4. Since Pythia does not yet integrate a reasoner, it approximates satisfiability checks by means of SPARQL queries. Whenever meaning representations are combined, it aggregates type information for the unified variable, together with selectional information connected to the occuring metavariables, and uses both to construct a SPARQL query. This query is then evaluated against the underlying knowledge base. If the query returns results, the interpetations are taken to be compatible, if it does not return results, the interpretations are taken to be incompatible and the according instantiation possibility of the metavariable is discarded. Note that those SPARQL queries are only an approximation for the OWL expressions used in 4.4. Furthermore, the results they return are only an approximation of satisfiability, as the reason for not returning results does not necessarily need to be unsatisfiability of the construction but could also be due the absence of data in the knowledge base. In order to overcome these shortcomings, we plan to integrate a full-fledged OWL reasoner in the future.

Out of the 880 user questions, 624 can be parsed by Pythia (for an evaluation on this dataset and reasons for failing with the remaining 256 questions, see (Unger & Cimiano, 2011)). Implementing the enumeration strategy, i.e. not using disambiguation mechanisms, there was a total of 3180 constructed queries. With a mechanism for removing scope ambiguities by means of simulating a linear scope preference, a total of 2936 queries was built. Additionally using the underspecification and resolution strategies described in the previous section, by exploiting the ontology with respect to which natural language expressions are interpreted in order to discard inconsistent interpretations as early as possible in the course of a derivation, the number of total queries was further reduced to 2100. This amounts to a reduction of the overall number of queries by 44 %. The average and maximum number of queries per question are summarized in the following table.

	Avg. # queries	Max. # queries
Enumeration	5.1	96
Linear scope	4.7 (-8%)	46 (-52%)
Reasoning	3.4 (-44%)	24 (-75%)

6 Conclusion

We investigated ambiguities arising from mismatches between a natural language expressions' lexical meaning and its conceptual modelling in an ontology. Employing ontological reasoning for disambiguation allowed us to significantly reduce the number of constructed interpretations: the average number of constructed queries per question can be reduced by 44 %, the maximum number of queries per question can be reduced even by 75 %.

References

Bunt, H.: Semantic Underspecification: Which Technique For What Purpose? In: Computing Meaning, vol. 83, pp. 55–85. Springer Netherlands (2007)

Cimiano, P.: Flexible semantic composition with DUDES. In: Proceedings of the 8th International Conference on Computational Semantics (IWCS). Tilburg (2009)

Unger, C., Hieber, F., Cimiano, P.: Generating LTAG grammars from a lexicon-ontology interface. In: S. Bangalore, R. Frank, and M. Romero (eds.): 10th International Workshop on Tree Adjoining Grammars and Related Formalisms (TAG+10), Yale University (2010)

Unger, C., Cimiano, P.: Pythia: Compositional meaning construction for ontology-based question answering on the Semantic Web. In: Proceedings of the 16th International Conference on Applications of Natural Language to Information Systems (NLDB) (2011)

Schabes, Y.: Mathematical and Computational Aspects of Lexicalized Grammars. Ph. D. thesis, University of Pennsylvania (1990)

Reyle, U.: Dealing with ambiguities by underspecification: Construction, representation and deduction. Journal of Semantics 10, 123–179 (1993)

Kamp, H., Reyle, U.: From Discourse to Logic. Kluwer, Dordrecht (1993)

Cimiano, P., Minock, M.: Natural Language Interfaces: What's the Problem? – A Data-driven Quantitative Analysis. In: Proceedings of the International Conference on Applications of Natural Language to Information Systems (NLDB), pp. 192–206 (2009)

Damljanovic, D., Agatonovic, M., Cunningham, H.: Natural Language Interfaces to Ontologies: Combining Syntactic Analysis and Ontology-based Lookup through the User Interaction. In: Proceedings of the 7th Extended Semantic Web Conference, Springer Verlag (2010)

Zettlemoyer, L., Collins, M.: Learning Context-dependent Mappings from Sentences to Logical Form. In: Proceedings of the Joint Conference of the Association for Computational Linguistics and International Joint Conference on Natural Language Processing (ACL-IJCNLP), pp. 976–984 (2009)

Burger, J., Cardie, C., Chaudhri, V., Gaizauskas, R., Israel, D., Jacquemin, C., Lin, C.-Y., Maiorano, S., Miller, G., Moldovan, D., Ogden, B., Prager, J., Riloff, E., Singhal, A., Shrihari, R., Strzalkowski, T., Voorhees, E., Weischedel, R.: Issues, tasks, and program structures to roadmap research in question & answering (Q & A). `http://www-nlpir.nist.gov/projects/duc/papers/qa.Roadmap-paper_v2.doc` (2001)

Kate, R., Mooney, R.: Learning Language Semantics from Ambiguous Supervision. In: Proceedings of the 22nd Conference on Artificial Intelligence (AAAI-07), pp. 895–900 (2007)

Strings over intervals

Tim Fernando
Computer Science Department
Trinity College, Dublin 2
Ireland
Tim.Fernando@tcd.ie

Abstract

Intervals and the events that occur in them are encoded as strings, elaborating on a conception of events as "intervals cum description." Notions of satisfaction in interval temporal logics are formulated in terms of strings, and the possibility of computing these via finite-state machines/transducers is investigated. This opens up temporal semantics to finite-state methods, with entailments that are decidable insofar as these can be reduced to inclusions between regular languages.

1 Introduction

It is well-known that Kripke models for *Linear Termporal Logic* (LTL) can be formulated as strings (e.g. Emerson, 1990). For the purposes of natural language semantics, however, it has been argued since at least (Bennett and Partee, 1972) that intervals should replace points. It is less clear (than in the case of LTL) how to view models as strings for intervals drawn (say) from the real line $\mathbb{R}$, as in one of the more recent interval temporal logics proposed for English, the system $\mathcal{TPL}$ of (Pratt-Hartmann, 2005). But if we follow $\mathcal{TPL}$ in restricting our models to finite sets, we can encode satisfaction of a formula ψ in a set $\mathcal{L}(\psi)$ of strings $str(\mathcal{A}, I)$ representing models $\mathcal{A}$ and intervals I

$$(\dagger) \qquad \mathcal{A} \models_I \psi \iff str(\mathcal{A}, I) \in \mathcal{L}(\psi)\ .$$

The present paper shows how to devise encodings $str(\mathcal{A}, I)$ and $\mathcal{L}(\psi)$ that establish ($\dagger$) in a way that opens temporal semantics up to finite-state methods (e.g. Beesley and Karttunen, 2003). Notice that the entailment from ψ to ψ' given by

$$(\forall \mathcal{A}, I) \quad \text{if } \mathcal{A} \models_I \psi \text{ then } \mathcal{A} \models_I \psi'$$

is equivalent, under ($\dagger$), to the inclusion $\mathcal{L}(\psi) \subseteq \mathcal{L}(\psi')$. This inclusion is decidable provided $\mathcal{L}(\psi)$ and $\mathcal{L}(\psi')$ are regular languages. (The same cannot be said for context-free languages.)

1.1 $\mathcal{TPL}$-models and strings

We start with $\mathcal{TPL}$, a model in which is defined, relative to an infinite set E of *event-atoms*, to be a finite set $\mathcal{A}$ of pairs $\langle I, e\rangle$ of closed, bounded intervals $I \subseteq \mathbb{R}$ and event-atoms $e \in E$. (A closed, bounded interval in $\mathbb{R}$ has the form

$$[r_1, r_2] \stackrel{\text{def}}{=} \{r \in \mathbb{R} \mid r_1 \leq r \leq r_2\}$$

for some $r_1, r_2 \in \mathbb{R}$.) The idea is that $\langle I, e\rangle$ represents "an occurrence of an event of type e over the interval" I (Pratt-Hartmann, 2005; page 17). That is, we can think of $\mathcal{A}$ as a finite set of events, conceived as "intervals cum description" (van Benthem, 1983; page 113). Our goal below is to string out this conception beyond event-atoms, and consider relations between intervals other than sub-intervalhood (the focus of $\mathcal{TPL}$). To get some sense for what is involved, it is useful to pause for examples of the strings we have in mind.[1]

[1] Concrete English examples connected with text inference can be found in (Pratt-Hartmann, 2005; Pratt-Hartmann, 2005a), the latter of which isolates a fragment $\mathcal{TPL}^*$ of $\mathcal{TPL}$ related specifically to TimeML (Pustejovsky et al., 2003). The finite-state encoding below pays off in expanding the coverage

$$\rho_X(\alpha_1 \cdots \alpha_n) \stackrel{\text{def}}{=} (\alpha_1 \cap X) \cdots (\alpha_n \cap X)$$

$$bc(\mathsf{s}) \stackrel{\text{def}}{=} \begin{cases} bc(\alpha \mathsf{s}') & \text{if } \mathsf{s} = \alpha\alpha\mathsf{s}' \\ \alpha bc(\alpha' \mathsf{s}') & \text{if } \mathsf{s} = \alpha\alpha'\mathsf{s}' \text{ and } \alpha \neq \alpha' \\ \mathsf{s} & \text{otherwise} \end{cases}$$

Table 1: Two useful functions

Example A Given event-atoms e and e', let $\mathcal{A}$ be the $\mathcal{TPL}$-model $\{x_1, x_2, x_3\}$, where

$$x_1 \stackrel{\text{def}}{=} \langle [1,4], e \rangle$$
$$x_2 \stackrel{\text{def}}{=} \langle [3,9], e \rangle$$
$$x_3 \stackrel{\text{def}}{=} \langle [9,100], e' \rangle \ .$$

Over the alphabet $Pow(\mathcal{A})$ of subsets of $\mathcal{A}$, let us represent $\mathcal{A}$ by the string

$$s(\mathcal{A}) \stackrel{\text{def}}{=} \boxed{x_1}\boxed{x_1, x_2}\boxed{x_2}\boxed{x_2, x_3}\boxed{x_3}$$

of length 5, each box representing a symbol (i.e. a subset of $\mathcal{A}$) and arranged in chronological order with time increasing from left to right much like a film/cartoon strip (Fernando, 2004). Precisely how $s(\mathcal{A})$ is constructed from $\mathcal{A}$ is explained in section 2. Lest we think that a box represents an indivisible instant of time, we turn quickly to

Example B The 12 months, January to December, in a year are represented by the string

$$s_{y/m} \stackrel{\text{def}}{=} \boxed{\text{Jan}}\boxed{\text{Feb}} \cdots \boxed{\text{Dec}}$$

of length 12, and the 365 days of a (common) year by the string

$$s_{y/m,d} \stackrel{\text{def}}{=} \boxed{\text{Jan,d1}}\boxed{\text{Jan,d2}} \cdots \boxed{\text{Dec,d31}}$$

of length 365. These two strings are linked by two functions on strings: a function ρ_{months} that keeps only the months in a box so that

$$\rho_{months}(s_{y/m,d}) = \boxed{\text{Jan}}^{31}\boxed{\text{Feb}}^{28} \cdots \boxed{\text{Dec}}^{31}$$

and *block compression* bc, which compresses consecutive occurrences of a box into one, mapping $\rho_{months}(s_{y/m,d})$ to

$$bc(\boxed{\text{Jan}}^{31}\boxed{\text{Feb}}^{28} \cdots \boxed{\text{Dec}}^{31}) = s_{y/m} \ .$$

to examples discussed in (Fernando, 2011a) and papers cited therein. These matters are given short shrift below (due to space and time constraints); I hope to make amends at my talk in the workshop.

(A_1)	$x \bigcirc x$	(i.e. $\bigcirc$ is reflexive)
(A_2)	$x \bigcirc x' \implies x' \bigcirc x$	
(A_3)	$x \prec x' \implies \text{not } x \bigcirc x'$	
(A_4)	$x \prec x' \bigcirc x'' \prec x''' \implies x \prec x'''$	
(A_5)	$x \prec x'$ or $x \bigcirc x'$ or $x' \prec x$	

Table 2: Axioms for event structures

That is,

$$bc(\rho_{months}(s_{y/m,d})) = s_{y/m}$$

where, as made precise in Table 1, ρ_X "sees only X" (equating *months* with {Jan, Feb, ... Dec} to make ρ_{months} an instance of ρ_X), while bc discards duplications, in accordance with the view that time passes only if there is change. Or rather: we observe time passing only if we observe a change in the contents of a box. The point of this example is that temporal granularity depends on the set X of what are observable — i.e., the *boxables* (we can put inside a box). That set X might be a $\mathcal{TPL}$-model $\mathcal{A}$ or more generally the set $\mathbf{E}$ of events in an *event structure* $\langle \mathbf{E}, \bigcirc, \prec \rangle$, as defined in (Kamp and Reyle, 1993).

Example C Given a $\mathcal{TPL}$-model $\mathcal{A}$, let $\bigcirc$ and $\prec$ be binary relations on $\mathcal{A}$ given by

$$\langle I, e \rangle \bigcirc \langle I', e' \rangle \stackrel{\text{def}}{\iff} I \cap I' \neq \emptyset$$
$$\langle I, e \rangle \prec \langle I', e' \rangle \stackrel{\text{def}}{\iff} (\forall r \in I)(\forall r' \in I')\ r < r'$$

for all $\langle I, e \rangle$ and $\langle I', e' \rangle \in \mathcal{A}$. Clearly, the triple $\langle \mathcal{A}, \bigcirc, \prec \rangle$ is an event structure — i.e., it satisfies axioms (A_1) to (A_5) in Table 2. But for finite $\mathcal{A}$, the temporal structure the real line $\mathbb{R}$ confers on $\mathcal{A}$ is reduced considerably by the Russell-Wiener-Kamp derivation of time from event structures (RWK). Indeed, for the particular $\mathcal{TPL}$-model $\mathcal{A}$ in Example A above, RWK yields exactly two temporal points, constituting the substring $\boxed{x_1, x_2}\boxed{x_2, x_3}$ of the string $s(\mathcal{A})$ of length 5. As an RWK-moment from an event structure $\langle \mathbf{E}, \bigcirc, \prec \rangle$ is required to be a $\subseteq$-maximal set of pairwise $\bigcirc$-overlapping events, RWK discards the three boxes $\boxed{x_1}$, $\boxed{x_2}$ and $\boxed{x_3}$ in $s(\mathcal{A})$. There is, however, a simple fix from (Fernando, 2011) that reconciles RWK not only with $s(\mathcal{A})$ but also with block compression bc: enlarge the set $\mathcal{A}$ of events/boxables to include *pre-* and *post-*

events, turning $s(\mathcal{A})$ into

$$\boxed{x_1, pre(x_2), pre(x_3)}\boxed{x_1, x_2, pre(x_3)}\boxed{x_2, post(x_1), pre(x_3)}\boxed{x_2, x_3, post(x_1)}\boxed{x_3, post(x_1), post(x_2)} .$$

Note that $pre(x_i)$ and $post(x_i)$ mark the past and future relative to x_i, injecting, in the terminology of (McTaggart, 1908), A-series ingredients for tense into the B-series relations $\prec$ and $\bigcirc$ (which is just $\prec$-incomparability). For our present purposes, these additional ingredients allow us to represent all 13 relations between intervals x and x' in (Allen, 1983) by event structures over $\{x, x', pre(x), post(x')\}$, including the sub-interval relation x *during* x' at the center of (Pratt-Hartmann, 2005),[2] which strings out to

$$\boxed{pre(x), x'}\boxed{x, x'}\boxed{post(x), x'} .$$

It will prove useful in our account of $\mathcal{TPL}$-formulas below to internalize the demarcation of x by $pre(x)$ and $post(x)$ when forming $str(\mathcal{A}, I)$.

1.2 Outline

The remainder of the paper is organized as follows. Section 2 fills in details left out in our presentation of examples above, supplying the ingredient $str(\mathcal{A}, I)$ in the equivalence

$$(\dagger) \qquad \mathcal{A} \models_I \psi \iff str(\mathcal{A}, I) \in \mathcal{L}(\psi) .$$

The equivalence itself is not established before section 3, where every $\mathcal{TPL}$-formula ψ is mapped to a language $\mathcal{L}(\psi)$ via a translation ψ_+ of ψ to a minor variant $\mathcal{TPL}_+$ of $\mathcal{TPL}$. That variant is designed to smoothen the step in section 4 from $\mathcal{TPL}$ to other interval temporal logics which can be strung out similarly, and can, under natural assumptions, be made amenable to finite-state methods.

[2] Or to be more correct, the version of $\mathcal{TPL}$ in (Pratt-Hartmann, 2005a), as the strict subset relation $\subset$ between intervals assumed in the *Artificial Intelligence* article amounts to the disjunction of the Allen relations *during*, *starts* and *finishes*. For concreteness, we work with $\subset$ below; only minor changes are required to switch to *during*.

2 Strings encoding finite interval models

This section forms the string $str(\mathcal{A}, I)$ in three stages described by the equation

$$str(\mathcal{A}, I) \stackrel{\text{def}}{=} s(\mathcal{A}_I)^\bullet .$$

First, we combine $\mathcal{A}$ and I into the restriction $\mathcal{A}_I$ of $\mathcal{A}$ to pairs $\langle J, e\rangle$ such that J is a strict subset of I

$$\mathcal{A}_I \stackrel{\text{def}}{=} \{\langle J, e\rangle \in \mathcal{A} \mid J \subset I\}$$

Second, we systematize the construction of the string $s(\mathcal{A})$ in Example A. And third, we map a string s to a string $s^\bullet$ that internalizes the borders externally marked by the *pre*- and *post*-events described in Example C. The map $\mathcal{A} \mapsto s(\mathcal{A})$ is the business of §2.1, and $s \mapsto s^\bullet$ of §2.2. With an eye to interval temporal logics other than $\mathcal{TPL}$, we will consider the full set $Ivl(\mathbb{R})$ of (non-empty) intervals in $\mathbb{R}$

$$Ivl(\mathbb{R}) \stackrel{\text{def}}{=} \{a \subseteq \mathbb{R} \mid a \neq \emptyset \text{ and } (\forall x, y \in a)\ [x, y] \subseteq a\} ,$$

and write $]r_1, r_2[$ for the open interval

$$]r_1, r_2[\stackrel{\text{def}}{=} \{r \in \mathbb{R} \mid r_1 < r < r_2\}$$

where we allow $r_1 = -\infty$ for intervals unbounded to the left and $r_2 = +\infty$ for intervals unbounded to the right. The constructs $\pm\infty$ are convenient for associating *endpoints* with every interval I, whether or not I is bounded. For I bounded to the left and to the right, we refer to real numbers r and r' as I's endpoints provided $I \subseteq [r, r']$ and

$$[r, r'] \subseteq [r'', r'''] \quad \text{for all } r'' \text{ and } r''' \text{ such that } I \subseteq [r'', r'''] .$$

We write $Endpoints(I)$ for the (non-empty) set consisting of I's endpoints (including possibly $\pm\infty$).

2.1 Order, box and compress

Given a finite subset $\mathcal{A} \subseteq Ivl(\mathbb{R}) \times E$, we collect all endpoints of intervals in $\mathcal{A}$ in the finite set

$$Endpoints(\mathcal{A}) \stackrel{\text{def}}{=} \bigcup_{\langle I,e\rangle \in \mathcal{A}} Endpoints(I)$$

and construct $s(\mathcal{A})$ in three steps.

Step 1 Order *Endpoints*($\mathcal{A}$) into an increasing sequence

$$r_1 < r_2 < \cdots < r_n.$$

Step 2 Box the $\mathcal{A}$-events into the sequence of $2n-1$ intervals

$$\{r_1\}, \,]r_1, r_2[, \,\{r_2\}, \,]r_2, r_3[, \,\ldots \{r_n\}$$

(partitioning the closed interval $[r_1, r_n]$), forming the string

$$\alpha_1\beta_1\alpha_2\beta_2 \cdots \alpha_n$$

(of length $2n-1$) where

$$\alpha_j \stackrel{\text{def}}{=} \{\langle i, e\rangle \in \mathcal{A} \mid r_j \in i\}$$
$$\beta_j \stackrel{\text{def}}{=} \{\langle i, e\rangle \in \mathcal{A} \mid]r_j, r_{j+1}[\subseteq i\}\ .$$

Step 3 Block-compress $\alpha_1\beta_1\alpha_2\beta_2 \cdots \alpha_n$

$$s(\mathcal{A}) \stackrel{\text{def}}{=} bc(\alpha_1\beta_1\alpha_2\beta_2 \cdots \alpha_n)\ .$$

For example, revisiting Example A, where $\mathcal{A}$ is $\{x_1, x_2, x_3\}$ and

$$x_1 \stackrel{\text{def}}{=} \langle [1,4], e\rangle$$
$$x_2 \stackrel{\text{def}}{=} \langle [3,9], e\rangle$$
$$x_3 \stackrel{\text{def}}{=} \langle [9,100], e'\rangle$$

we have from Step 1, the 5 endpoints

$$\vec{r} = 1, 3, 4, 9, 100$$

and from Step 2, the 9 boxes

$$\boxed{x_1}\boxed{x_1}\boxed{x_1, x_2}\boxed{x_1, x_2}\boxed{x_1, x_2}\boxed{x_2}\boxed{x_2, x_3}\boxed{x_3}\boxed{x_3}$$

that block-compresses in Step 3 to the 5 boxes $s(\mathcal{A})$

$$\boxed{x_1}\boxed{x_1, x_2}\boxed{x_2}\boxed{x_2, x_3}\boxed{x_3}\ .$$

Notice that if we turned the closed intervals in x_1 and x_3 to open intervals $]1, 4[$ and $]9, 100[$ respectively, then Step 2 gives

$$\boxed{}\boxed{x_1}\boxed{x_1, x_2}\boxed{x_1, x_2}\boxed{x_2}\boxed{x_2}\boxed{x_2}\boxed{x_3}\boxed{}$$

which block-compresses to the 6 boxes

$$\boxed{}\boxed{x_1}\boxed{x_1, x_2}\boxed{x_2}\boxed{x_3}\boxed{}\ .$$

2.2 Demarcated events

Block compression accounts for part of the Russell-Wiener-Kamp constuction of moments from an event structure (RWK). We can neutralize the requirement of $\subseteq$-maximality on RWK moments by adding $pre(x_i), post(x_i)$, turning, for instance, $s(\mathcal{A})$ for $\mathcal{A}$ given by Example A into

$$\boxed{x_1, pre(x_2), pre(x_3)}\boxed{x_1, x_2, pre(x_3)}$$
$$\boxed{post(x_1), x_2, pre(x_3)}\boxed{post(x_1), x_2, x_3}$$
$$\boxed{post(x_1), post(x_2), x_3}$$

(which $\rho_{\mathcal{A}}$ maps back to $s(\mathcal{A})$). In general, we say a string $\alpha_1\alpha_2 \cdots \alpha_n$ is *$\mathcal{A}$-delimited* if for all $x \in \mathcal{A}$ and integers i from 1 to n,

$$pre(x) \in \alpha_i \iff x \in (\bigcup_{j=i+1}^{n} \alpha_j) - \bigcup_{j=1}^{i} \alpha_j$$

and

$$post(x) \in \alpha_i \iff x \in (\bigcup_{j=1}^{i-1} \alpha_j) - \bigcup_{j=i}^{n} \alpha_j\ .$$

Clearly, for every string $s \in Pow(\mathcal{A})^*$, there is a unique $\mathcal{A}$-delimited string s' such that $\rho_{\mathcal{A}}(s') = s$. Let $s_{\pm}$ be that unique string.

Notice that $pre(x)$ and $post(x)$ explicitly mark the borders of x in $s_{\pm}$. For the application at hand to $\mathcal{TPL}$, it is useful to internalize the borders within x so that, for instance in Example A, $s(\mathcal{A})_{\pm}$ becomes

$$\boxed{x_1, begin\text{-}x_1}\boxed{x_1, x_2, x_1\text{-}end, begin\text{-}x_2}$$
$$\boxed{x_2}\boxed{x_2, x_3, x_2\text{-}end, begin\text{-}x_3}\boxed{x_3, x_3\text{-}end}$$

(with $pre(x_i)$ shifted to the right as *begin-*x_i and $post(x_i)$ to the left as x_i*-end*). The general idea is that given a string $\alpha_1\alpha_2 \cdots \alpha_n \in Pow(\mathcal{A})^n$ and $x \in \mathcal{A}$ that occurs at some α_i, we add *begin-*x to the first box in which x appears, and x*-end* to the last box in which x appears. Or economizing a bit by picking out the first component *I* in a pair $\langle I, e\rangle \in \mathcal{A}$, we form the *demarcation* $(\alpha_1\alpha_2 \cdots \alpha_n)^\bullet$ of $\alpha_1\alpha_2 \cdots \alpha_n$ by adding *bgn-I* to α_i precisely if

> there is some e such that $\langle I, e\rangle \in \alpha_i$ and either $i = 1$ or $\langle I, e\rangle \notin \alpha_{i-1}$

$$\begin{aligned}\varphi &::= mult(e) \mid \neg\varphi \mid \varphi \wedge \varphi' \mid \langle\beta\rangle\varphi \\ \alpha &::= e \mid e^f \mid e^l \\ \beta &::= \alpha \mid \alpha^< \mid \alpha^>\end{aligned}$$

Table 3: $\mathcal{TPL}_+$-formulas φ from extended labels β

and adding I-*end* to α_i precisely if

> there is some e such that $\langle I, e\rangle \in \alpha_i$ and either $i = n$ or $\langle I, e\rangle \notin \alpha_{i+1}$.

Returning to Example A, we have

$$s(\mathcal{A})^\bullet = \boxed{x_1, bgn\text{-}I_1} \boxed{x_1, x_2, I_1\text{-}end, bgn\text{-}I_2} \boxed{x_2} \boxed{x_2, x_3, I_2\text{-}end, bgn\text{-}I_3} \boxed{x_3, I_3\text{-}end}$$

which is $str(\mathcal{A}, I)$ for any interval I such that $[1, 100] \subset I$.

3 $\mathcal{TPL}$-satisfaction in terms of strings

This section defines the set $\mathcal{L}(\psi)$ of strings for the equivalence (†)

$$(\dagger) \qquad \mathcal{A} \models_I \psi \iff str(\mathcal{A}, I) \in \mathcal{L}(\psi)$$

by a translation to a language $\mathcal{TPL}_+$ that differs ever so slightly from $\mathcal{TPL}$ and its extension $\mathcal{TPL}^+$ in (Pratt-Hartmann, 2005). As in $\mathcal{TPL}$ and $\mathcal{TPL}^+$, formulas in $\mathcal{TPL}_+$ are closed under the modal operator $\langle e\rangle$, for every event-atom $e \in E$. Essentially, $\langle e\rangle\top$ says at least one e-transition is possible. In addition, $\mathcal{TPL}_+$ has a formula $mult(e)$ stating that multiple (at least two) e-transitions are possible. That is, $mult(e)$ amounts to the $\mathcal{TPL}^+$-formula

$$\langle e\rangle\top \wedge \neg\{e\}\top$$

where the $\mathcal{TPL}^+$-formula $\{e\}\psi$ can be rephrased as

$$\langle e\rangle\psi \wedge \neg mult(e)$$

(and $\top$ as the tautology $\neg(mult(e) \wedge \neg mult(e))$). More formally, $\mathcal{TPL}_+$-formulas φ are generated according to Table 3 without any explicit mention of the $\mathcal{TPL}$-constructs $\{\alpha\}$, $\{\alpha\}_<$ and $\{\alpha\}_>$. Instead, a $\mathcal{TPL}^+$-formula ψ is translated to a $\mathcal{TPL}_+$-formula ψ_+ so that (†) holds with $\mathcal{L}(\psi)$ equal to $\mathcal{T}(\psi_+)$, where $\mathcal{T}(\varphi)$ is a set of strings (defined below) characterizing satisfaction in $\mathcal{TPL}_+$. The translation ψ_+ commutes with the connectives common to $\mathcal{TPL}^+$ and $\mathcal{TPL}_+$

$$\text{e.g., } (\neg\psi)_+ \stackrel{\text{def}}{=} \neg(\psi_+)$$

and elsewhere,

$$\begin{aligned}\top_+ &\stackrel{\text{def}}{=} \neg(mult(e) \wedge \neg mult(e)) \\ (\{e\}\psi)_+ &\stackrel{\text{def}}{=} \langle e\rangle\psi_+ \wedge \neg mult(e) \\ ([e]\psi)_+ &\stackrel{\text{def}}{=} \neg\langle e\rangle\neg\psi_+ \\ (\{e\}_<\psi)_+ &\stackrel{\text{def}}{=} \langle e^<\rangle\psi_+ \wedge \neg mult(e) \\ (\{e\}_>\psi)_+ &\stackrel{\text{def}}{=} \langle e^>\rangle\psi_+ \wedge \neg mult(e)\end{aligned}$$

and as minimal-first and minimal-last subintervals are unique (Pratt-Hartmann, 2005, page 18),

$$\begin{aligned}(\{e^g\}_<\psi)_+ &\stackrel{\text{def}}{=} \langle e^{g<}\rangle\psi_+ \text{ for } g \in \{f, l\} \\ (\{e^g\}_>\psi)_+ &\stackrel{\text{def}}{=} \langle e^{g>}\rangle\psi_+ \text{ for } g \in \{f, l\} .\end{aligned}$$

3.1 The alphabet $\Sigma = \Sigma_{\mathfrak{I},E}$ and its subscripts

The alphabet from which we form strings will depend on a choice $\mathfrak{I}, E$ of a set $\mathfrak{I} \subseteq Ivl(\mathbb{R})$ of real intervals, and a set E of event-atoms. Recalling that the demarcation $s(\mathcal{A})^\bullet$ of a string $s(\mathcal{A})$ contains occurrences of bgn-I and I-end, for each $I \in domain(\mathcal{A})$, let us associate with $\mathfrak{I}$ the set

$$\mathfrak{I}_\bullet \stackrel{\text{def}}{=} \{bgn\text{-}I \mid I \in \mathfrak{I}\} \cup \{I\text{-}end \mid I \in \mathfrak{I}\}$$

from which we build the alphabet

$$\Sigma_{\mathfrak{I},E} \stackrel{\text{def}}{=} Pow((\mathfrak{I} \times E) \cup \mathfrak{I}_\bullet)$$

so that a symbol (i.e., element of $\Sigma_{\mathfrak{I},E}$) is a set with elements of the form $\langle I, e\rangle$, bgn-I and I-end. Notice that

$$(\forall \mathcal{A} \subseteq \mathfrak{I} \times E) \qquad str(\mathcal{A}, I) \in \Sigma^*_{\mathfrak{I},E}$$

for any real interval I. To simplify notation, we will often drop the subscripts $\mathfrak{I}$ and E, restoring them when we have occasion to vary them. This applies not only to the alphabet $\Sigma = \Sigma_{\mathfrak{I},E}$ but also to the truth sets $\mathcal{T}(\psi) = \mathcal{T}_{\mathfrak{I},E}(\psi)$ below, with $\mathfrak{I}$ fixed in the case of (†) to the full set of closed, bounded real intervals.

3.2 The truth sets $\mathcal{T}(\varphi)$

We start with *mult*(e), the truth set $\mathcal{T}(mult(e))$ for which consists of strings properly containing at least two e-events. We first clarify what "properly contain" means, before turning to "e-events." The notion of containment needed combines two ways a string can be part of another. The first involves deleting some (possibly null) prefix and suffix of a string. A *factor of* a string s is a string s' such that $s = us'v$ for some strings u and v, in which case we write $s\ fac\ s'$

$$s\ fac\ s' \stackrel{\text{def}}{\iff} (\exists u, v)\ s = us'v\ .$$

A factor of s is *proper* if it is distinct from s. That is, writing $s\ pfac\ s'$ to mean s' is a proper factor of s,

$$s\ pfac\ s' \iff (\exists u, v)\ s = us'v \text{ and } uv \neq \epsilon$$

where ϵ is the null string. The relation *pfac* between strings corresponds roughly to that of proper inclusion $\supset$ between intervals.

The second notion of part between strings applies specifically to strings s and s' of sets: we say s *subsumes* s', and write $s \trianglerighteq s'$, if they are of the same length, and $\supseteq$ holds componentwise between them

$$\alpha_1 \cdots \alpha_n \trianglerighteq \alpha'_1 \cdots \alpha'_m \stackrel{\text{def}}{\iff} n = m \text{ and } \alpha'_i \subseteq \alpha_i \text{ for } 1 \leq i \leq n$$

(Fernando, 2004). Now, writing $R; R'$ for the *composition of* binary relations R and R' in which the output of R is fed as input to R'

$$s\ R; R'\ s' \stackrel{\text{def}}{\iff} (\exists s'')\ sRs'' \text{ and } s''R's'\ ,$$

we compose *fac* with $\trianglerighteq$ for *containment* $\sqsupseteq$

$$\sqsupseteq \ \stackrel{\text{def}}{=}\ fac\ ;\ \trianglerighteq \qquad (= \trianglerighteq\ ;\ fac)$$

and *pfac* with $\trianglerighteq$ for *proper containment* $\sqsupset$

$$\sqsupset \ \stackrel{\text{def}}{=}\ pfac\ ;\ \trianglerighteq \qquad (= \trianglerighteq\ ;\ pfac)\ .$$

Next, for e-events, given $I \in \mathfrak{I}$, let

$$\mathcal{D}(e, I) \stackrel{\text{def}}{=} \{s^{\bullet} \mid s \in \boxed{\langle I, e\rangle}^{+}\}$$

and summing over intervals $I \in \mathfrak{I}$,

$$\mathcal{D}_{\mathfrak{I}}(e) \stackrel{\text{def}}{=} \bigcup_{I \in \mathfrak{I}} \mathcal{D}(e, I)\ .$$

Dropping the subscripts on Σ and $\mathcal{D}(e)$, we put into $\mathcal{T}(mult(e))$ all strings in Σ^* properly containing more than one string in $\mathcal{D}(e)$

$$s \in \mathcal{T}(mult(e)) \stackrel{\text{def}}{\iff} (\exists s_1, s_2 \in \mathcal{D}(e))\ s_1 \neq s_2 \text{ and } s \sqsupset s_1 \text{ and } s \sqsupset s_2.$$

Moving on, we interpret negation $\neg$ and conjunction $\wedge$ classically

$$\mathcal{T}(\neg\varphi) \stackrel{\text{def}}{=} \Sigma^* - \mathcal{T}(\varphi)$$
$$\mathcal{T}(\varphi \wedge \varphi') \stackrel{\text{def}}{=} \mathcal{T}(\varphi) \cap \mathcal{T}(\varphi')$$

and writing $R^{-1}L$ for $\{s \in \Sigma^* \mid (\exists s' \in L)\ sRs'\}$, we set

$$\mathcal{T}(\langle\beta\rangle\varphi) \stackrel{\text{def}}{=} \mathcal{R}(\beta)^{-1}\mathcal{T}(\varphi)$$

which brings us to the question of $\mathcal{R}(\beta)$.

3.3 The accessibility relations $\mathcal{R}(\beta)$

Having defined $\mathcal{T}(mult(e))$, we let $\mathcal{R}(e)$ be the restriction of proper containment $\sqsupset$ to $\mathcal{D}(e)$

$$s\ \mathcal{R}(e)\ s' \stackrel{\text{def}}{\iff} s \sqsupset s' \text{ and } s' \in \mathcal{D}(e)\ .$$

As for e^f and e^l, some preliminary notation is useful. Given a language L, let us collect strings that have at most one factor in L in *nmf*(L) (for *n*on-*m*ultiple *f*actor)

$$nmf(L) \stackrel{\text{def}}{=} \{s \in \Sigma^* \mid \text{at most one factor of } s \text{ belongs to } L\}$$

and let us shorten $\trianglerighteq^{-1}L$ to $L^{\trianglerighteq}$

$$s \in L^{\trianglerighteq} \stackrel{\text{def}}{\iff} (\exists s' \in L)\ s \trianglerighteq s'\ .$$

Now,

$$s\ \mathcal{R}(e^f)\ s' \stackrel{\text{def}}{\iff} (\exists u, v)\ s = us'v \text{ and } uv \neq \epsilon \text{ and } s' \in \mathcal{D}(e)^{\trianglerighteq} \text{ and } us' \in nmf(\mathcal{D}(e)^{\trianglerighteq})$$

and similarly,

$$s\,\mathcal{R}(e^l)\,s' \;\overset{\text{def}}{\iff}\; (\exists u,v)\; s = us'v \text{ and } uv \neq \epsilon \text{ and } s' \in \mathcal{D}(e)^{\unrhd} \text{ and } s'v \in nmf(\mathcal{D}(e)^{\unrhd})\,.$$

Finally,

$$s\,\mathcal{R}(\alpha^<)\,s' \;\overset{\text{def}}{\iff}\; (\exists s'',s''')\; s = s's''s''' \text{ and } s\,\mathcal{R}(\alpha)\,s''$$

$$s\,\mathcal{R}(\alpha^>)\,s' \;\overset{\text{def}}{\iff}\; (\exists s'',s''')\; s = s'''s''s' \text{ and } s\,\mathcal{R}(\alpha)\,s''\,.$$

A routine induction on $\mathcal{TPL}^+$-formulas ψ establishes that for $\mathfrak{I}$ equal to the set $\mathcal{I}$ of all closed, bounded real intervals,

Proposition 1. *For all finite $\mathcal{A} \subseteq \mathcal{I} \times E$ and $I \in \mathcal{I}$,*

$$\mathcal{A} \models_I \psi \iff str(\mathcal{A}, I) \in \mathcal{T}_{\mathcal{I},E}(\psi_+)$$

for every $\mathcal{TPL}^+$-formula ψ.

3.4 $\mathcal{TPL}$-equivalence and $\mathfrak{I}$ revisited

When do two pairs $\mathcal{A}, I$ and $\mathcal{A}', I'$ of finite subsets $\mathcal{A}, \mathcal{A}'$ of $\mathcal{I} \times E$ and intervals $I, I' \in \mathcal{I}$ satisfy the same $\mathcal{TPL}$-formulas? A sufficient condition suggested by Proposition 1 is that $str(\mathcal{A}, I)$ is the same as $str(\mathcal{A}', I')$ up to renaming of intervals. More precisely, recalling that $str(\mathcal{A}, I) = s(\mathcal{A}_I)^\bullet$, let us define $\mathcal{A}$ to be *congruent with* $\mathcal{A}'$, $\mathcal{A} \cong \mathcal{A}'$, if there is a bijection between the intervals of $\mathcal{A}$ and $\mathcal{A}'$ that turns $s(\mathcal{A})$ into $s(\mathcal{A}')$

$$\mathcal{A} \cong \mathcal{A}' \;\overset{\text{def}}{\iff}\; (\exists f : domain(\mathcal{A}) \to domain(\mathcal{A}'))\; f \text{ is a bijection, and } \mathcal{A}' = \{\langle f(I), e\rangle \mid \langle I, e\rangle \in \mathcal{A}\} \text{ and } f[s(\mathcal{A})] = s(\mathcal{A}')$$

where for any string $s \in Pow(domain(f) \times E)^*$,

$$f[s] \;\overset{\text{def}}{=}\; s \text{ after renaming each } I \in domain(f) \text{ to } f(I)\,.$$

As a corollary to Proposition 1, we have

Proposition 2. *For all finite subsets $\mathcal{A}$ and $\mathcal{A}'$ of $\mathcal{I} \times E$ and all $I, I' \in \mathcal{I}$, if $\mathcal{A}_I \cong \mathcal{A}'_{I'}$ then for every $\mathcal{TPL}^+$-formula ψ,*

$$\mathcal{A} \models_I \psi \iff \mathcal{A}' \models_{I'} \psi\,.$$

The significance of Proposition 2 is that it spells out the role the real line $\mathbb{R}$ plays in $\mathcal{TPL}$ — nothing apart from its contribution to the strings $s(\mathcal{A})$. Instead of picking out particular intervals over $\mathbb{R}$, it suffices to work with interval symbols, and to equate the subscript $\mathfrak{I}$ on our alphabet Σ and truth relations $\mathcal{T}(\psi)$ to say, the set $\mathbb{Z}_+$ of positive integers $1, 2, \ldots$. But lest we confuse $\mathcal{TPL}$ with Linear Temporal Logic, note that the usual order on $\mathbb{Z}_+$ does *not* shape the accessibility relations in $\mathcal{TPL}$. We use $\mathbb{Z}_+$ here only because it is big enough to include any finite subset $\mathcal{A}$ of $\mathcal{I} \times E$.

Turning to entailments, we can reduce entailments

$$\psi \vdash_{\mathcal{I},E} \psi' \;\overset{\text{def}}{\iff}\; (\forall \text{ finite } \mathcal{A} \subseteq \mathcal{I} \times E)(\forall I \in \mathcal{I})\; \mathcal{A} \models_I \psi \text{ implies } \mathcal{A} \models_I \psi'$$

to satisfiability as usual

$$\psi \vdash_{\mathcal{I},E} \psi' \iff \mathcal{T}_{\mathcal{I},E}(\psi \wedge \neg\psi') = \emptyset\,.$$

The basis of the decidability/complexity results in (Pratt-Hartmann, 2005) is a lemma (number 3 in page 20) that, for any $\mathcal{TPL}^+$-formula ψ, bounds the size of a minimal model of ψ. That is, as far as the satisfiability of a $\mathcal{TPL}^+$-formula ψ is concerned, we can reduce the subscript $\mathfrak{I}$ on $\mathcal{T}(\psi)$ to a finite set — or in the aforementioned reformulation, to a finite segment $\{1, 2, \ldots, n\}$ of $\mathbb{Z}_+$. We shall consider an even more drastic approach in the next section. For now, notice that the shift from the real line $\mathbb{R}$ towards strings conforms with

The Proposal of (Steedman, 2005)

> *the so-called temporal semantics of natural language is not primarily to do with time at all. Instead, the formal devices we need are those related to representation of causality and goal-directed action.* [p ix]

The idea is to move away from some absolute (independently given) notion of time (be they points or intervals) to the changes and forces that make natural language temporal.

4 The regularity of $\mathcal{TPL}$ and beyond

Having reformulated $\mathcal{TPL}$ in terms of strings, we proceed now to investigate the prospects for a finite-state approach to temporal semantics building on that reformulation. We start by bringing out the finite-state character of the connectives in $\mathcal{TPL}$ before considering some extensions.

4.1 $\mathcal{TPL}_+$-connectives are regular

It is well-known that the family of regular languages is closed under complementation and intersection — operations interpreting negation and conjunction, respectively. The point of this subsection is to show that all the $\mathcal{TPL}_+$-connectives map regular languages and regular relations to regular languages and regular relations. A relation is *regular* if it is computed by a finite-state transducer. If $\mathfrak{I}$ and E are both finite, then $\mathcal{D}_{\mathfrak{I},E}(e)$ is a regular language and $\sqsupset$ is a regular relation. Writing R_L for the relation $\{(s,s') \in R \mid s' \in L\}$, note that

$$\mathcal{R}(e) \quad = \quad \sqsupset_{\mathcal{D}(e)}$$

and that in general, if R and L are regular, then so is R_L.

Moving on, the set of strings with at least two factors belonging to L is

$$\mathit{twice}(L) \stackrel{\text{def}}{=} \Sigma^*(L\Sigma^* \cap (\Sigma^+ L\Sigma^*)) + \Sigma^*(L\Sigma^+ \cap L)\Sigma^*$$

and the set of strings that have a proper factor belonging to L is

$$[L] \stackrel{\text{def}}{=} \Sigma^+ L\Sigma^* + \Sigma^* L\Sigma^+ .$$

It follows that we can capture the set of strings that properly contain at least two strings in L as

$$\mathit{Mult}(L) \stackrel{\text{def}}{=} [\mathit{twice}(L^{\trianglerighteq})] .$$

Note that

$$\mathcal{T}(\mathit{mult}(e)) \quad = \quad \mathit{Mult}(\mathcal{D}(e))$$

and recalling $\mathcal{R}(e^f)$ and $\mathcal{R}(e^l)$ use *nmf*,

$$\mathit{nmf}(L) \quad = \quad \Sigma^* - \mathit{twice}(L) .$$

$\mathcal{R}(e^f)$ is $\mathit{minFirst}(\mathcal{D}(e)^{\trianglerighteq})$ where

$$s\ \mathit{minFirst}(L)\ s' \stackrel{\text{def}}{\iff} (\exists u,v)\ s = us'v \text{ and } uv \neq \epsilon \text{ and } s' \in L \text{ and } us' \in \mathit{nmf}(L)$$

and $\mathcal{R}(e^l)$ is $\mathit{minLast}(\mathcal{D}(e)^{\trianglerighteq})$ where

$$s\ \mathit{minLast}(L)\ s' \stackrel{\text{def}}{\iff} (\exists u,v)\ s = us'v \text{ and } uv \neq \epsilon \text{ and } s' \in L \text{ and } s'v \in \mathit{nmf}(L).$$

Finally, $\mathcal{R}(\alpha^<)$ is $\mathit{init}(\mathcal{R}(\alpha))$ where

$$s\ \mathit{init}(R)\ s' \stackrel{\text{def}}{\iff} (\exists s'', s''')\ s = s's''s''' \text{ and } s\ R\ s''$$

while $\mathcal{R}(\alpha^>)$ is $\mathit{fin}(\mathcal{R}(\alpha))$ where

$$s\ \mathit{fin}(R)\ s' \stackrel{\text{def}}{\iff} (\exists s'', s''')\ s = s'''s''s' \text{ and } s\ R\ s'' .$$

Proposition 3. *If L is a regular language and R is a regular relation, then*

(i) $\mathit{Mult}(L)$, $R^{-1}L$, and $\mathit{nmf}(L)$ are regular languages

(ii) R_L, $\mathit{minFirst}(L)$, $\mathit{minLast}(L)$, $\mathit{init}(R)$ and $\mathit{fin}(R)$ are regular relations.

4.2 Beyond sub-intervals

As is clear from the relations $\mathcal{R}(e)$, $\mathcal{TPL}$ makes do with the sub-interval relation $\sqsubset$ and a "quasi-guarded" fragment at that (Pratt-Hartmann, 2005, page 5). To string out the interval temporal logic $\mathcal{HS}$ (Halpern and Shoham, 1991), the key is to combine $\mathcal{A}$ and I using some $r \notin E$ to mark I (rather than forming $\mathcal{A}_I$)

$$\mathcal{A}_r[I] \stackrel{\text{def}}{=} \mathcal{A} \cup \{\langle I, r\rangle\}$$

and modify $\mathit{str}(\mathcal{A}, I)$ to define

$$\mathit{str}_r(\mathcal{A}, I) \stackrel{\text{def}}{=} s(\mathcal{A}_r[I])^\bullet .$$

Let us agree that (i) a string $\alpha_1 \cdots \alpha_n$ *r-marks* I if $\langle I, r\rangle \in \bigcup_{i=1}^{n} \alpha_i$, and that (ii) a string is *r-marked* if there is a unique I that it r-marks. For every r-marked string s, we define two strings: let $s \upharpoonright r$ be the factor of s with *bgn-I* in its first box and *I-end* in its last, where s r-marks I; and let s_{-r} be $\rho_{\Sigma}(s \upharpoonright r)$.[3] We can devise a finite-state transducer converting r-marked strings s into s_{-r}, which we can then apply to evaluate an event-atom e as an $\mathcal{HS}$-formula

$$s \in \mathcal{T}_r(e) \quad \overset{\text{def}}{\iff} \quad (\exists s' \in \mathcal{D}(e))\; s_{-r} \trianglerighteq s' \,.$$

It is also not difficult to build finite-state transducers for the accessibility relations $\mathcal{R}_r(\mathrm{B})$,$\mathcal{R}_r(\mathrm{E})$, $\mathcal{R}_r(\overline{\mathrm{B}})$, and $\mathcal{R}_r(\overline{\mathrm{E}})$, showing that, as in $\mathcal{TPL}$, the connectives in $\mathcal{HS}$ map regular languages and regular relations to regular languages and regular relations. The question for both $\mathcal{TPL}$ and $\mathcal{HS}$ is can we start with regular languages $\mathcal{D}(e)$? As noted towards the end of section 3, one way is to reduce the set $\mathfrak{I}$ of intervals to a finite set. We close with an alternative.

4.3 A modest proposal: splitting event-atoms

An alternative to $\mathcal{D}(e) = \bigcup_{I \in \mathfrak{I}} \mathcal{D}(e, I)$ is to ask what it is that makes an e-event an e-event, and encode that answer in $\mathcal{D}(e)$. In and of itself, an interval [3,9] cannot make $\langle [3,9], e\rangle$ an e-event, because in and of itself, $\langle [3,9], e\rangle$ is *not* an e-event. $\langle [3,9], e\rangle$ is an e-event only *in* a model $\mathcal{A}$ such that $\mathcal{A}([3,9], e)$.

Putting $\mathfrak{I}$ aside, let us suppose, for instance, that e were the event *Pat swim a mile*. We can represent the "internal temporal contour" of e through a parametrized temporal proposition $f(r)$ with parameter r ranging over the reals in the unit interval $[0, 1]$, and $f(r)$ saying *Pat has swum* r·*(a mile)*. Let $\mathcal{D}(e)$ be

$$\boxed{f(0)}\,\boxed{f_{\uparrow}}^{+}\,\boxed{f(1)}$$

where $f_{\uparrow}$ abbreviates the temporal proposition

$$(\exists r < 1)\; f(r) \wedge \textit{Previously}\, \neg f(r) \,.$$

[3] Σ is defined as in §3.1, and ρ_X as in §1.1 above. Were we to weaken $\subset$ to $\subseteq$ in the definition of $\mathcal{A}_I$ and the semantics of $\mathcal{TPL}$, then we would have $(\mathit{str}_r(\mathcal{A}, I))_{-r} = \mathit{str}(\mathcal{A}, I)$, and truth sets $\mathcal{T}_r(\varphi)$ and accessibility relations $\mathcal{R}_r(\beta)$ such that

$$\begin{aligned} \mathcal{T}(\varphi) &= \{ s_{-r} \mid s \in \mathcal{T}_r(\varphi) \} \\ \mathcal{R}(\beta) &= \{ \langle s_{-r}, s'_{-r} \rangle \mid s\, \mathcal{R}_r(\beta)\, s' \} \end{aligned}$$

for $\mathcal{TPL}_{+}$-formulas φ and extended labels β.

Notice that the temporal propositions $f(r)$ and $f_{\uparrow}$ are to be interpreted over points (as in LTL); as illustrated in Example B above, however, these points can be split by adding boxables. Be that as it may, it is straightforward to adjust our definition of a model $\mathcal{A}$ and $\mathit{str}_r(\mathcal{A}, I)$ to accommodate such changes to $\mathcal{D}(e)$. Basing the truth sets $\mathcal{T}(\varphi)$ on sets $\mathcal{D}(e)$ of e-denotations independent of a model $\mathcal{A}$ (Fernando, 2011a) is in line with the proposal of (Steedman, 2005) mentioned at the end of §3.4 above.

References

James F. Allen. 1983. Maintaining knowledge about temporal intervals. *Communications of the Association for Computing Machinery* 26(11): 832–843.

Kenneth R. Beesley and Lauri Karttunen. 2003. *Finite State Morphology*. CSLI, Stanford, CA.

Michael Bennett and Barbara Partee. 1972. Toward the logic of tense and aspect in English. Indiana University Linguistics Club, Bloomington, IN.

J.F.A.K. van Benthem. 1983. *The Logic of Time*. Reidel.

E. Allen Emerson. 1990. Temporal and modal logic. In (J. van Leeuwen, ed.) *Handbook of Theoretical Computer Science*, volume B. MIT Press, 995–1072.

Tim Fernando. 2004. A finite-state approach to events in natural langue semantics. *J. Logic & Comp* 14:79–92.

Tim Fernando. 2011. Constructing situations and time. *J. Philosophical Logic* 40(3):371–396.

Tim Fernando. 2011a. Regular relations for temporal propositions. *Natural Language Engineering* 17(2): 163–184.

Joseph Y. Halpern and Yoav Shoham. 1991. A Propositional Modal Logic of Time Intervals. *J. Association for Computing Machinery* 38(4): 935–962.

Hans Kamp and Uwe Reyle. 1993. *From Discourse to Logic*. Kluwer, Dordrecht.

John E. McTaggart. 1908. The Unreality of Time. *Mind* 17:456–473.

Ian Pratt-Hartmann. 2005. Temporal prepositions and their logic. *Artificial Intelligence* 166: 1–36.

Ian Pratt-Hartmann. 2005a. From TimeML to TPL*. In (G. Katz et al., eds.) *Annotating, Extracting and Reasoning about Time and Events*, Schloss Dagstuhl.

James Pustejovsky, José Castaño, Robert Ingria, Roser Saurí, Robert Gaizauskas, Andrea Setzer and Graham Katz. 2003. TimeML: Robust Specification of Event and Temporal Expressions in Text. In *5th International Workshop on Computational Semantics*. Tilburg.

Mark Steedman. 2005. The Productions of Time: Temporality and Causality in Linguistic Semantics. Draft, homepages.inf.ed.ac.uk/steedman/papers.html.

Discovering Commonsense Entailment Rules Implicit in Sentences

Jonathan Gordon
Department of Computer Science
University of Rochester
Rochester, NY, USA
jgordon@cs.rochester.edu

Lenhart K. Schubert
Department of Computer Science
University of Rochester
Rochester, NY, USA
schubert@cs.rochester.edu

Abstract

Reasoning about ordinary human situations and activities requires the availability of diverse types of knowledge, including expectations about the probable results of actions and the lexical entailments for many predicates. We describe initial work to acquire such a collection of conditional (if–then) knowledge by exploiting presuppositional discourse patterns (such as ones involving 'but', 'yet', and 'hoping to') and abstracting the matched material into general rules.

1 Introduction

We are interested, ultimately, in enabling an inference system to reason forward from facts as well as backward from goals, using lexical knowledge together with world knowledge. Creating appropriate collections of general world knowledge to support reasoning has long been a goal of researchers in Artificial Intelligence. Efforts in information extraction, *e.g.*, Banko *et al.* (2007), have focused on learning base facts about specific entities (such as that Barack Obama is president), and work in knowledge extraction, *e.g.*, Van Durme and Schubert (2008), has found generalizations (such as that a president may make a speech). While the latter provides a basis for possibilistic forward inference (Barack Obama probably makes a speech at least occasionally) when its meaning is sharpened (Gordon and Schubert, 2010), these resources don't provide a basis for saying what we might expect to happen if, for instance, someone crashes their car.

That the driver in a car crash might be injured and the car damaged is a matter of common sense, and, as such, is rarely stated directly. However, it can be found in sentences where this expectation is disconfirmed: 'Sally crashed her car into a tree, but she wasn't hurt.' We have been exploring the use of lexico-syntactic discourse patterns indicating disconfirmed expectations, as well as people's goals ('Joe apologized repeatedly, hoping to be forgiven'). The resulting rules, expressed at this point in natural language, are a first step toward obtaining classes of general conditional knowledge typically not obtained by other methods.

2 Related Work

One well-known approach to conditional knowledge acquisition is that of Lin and Pantel (2001), where inference rules are learned using distributional similarity between dependency tree paths. These results include entailment rules like 'x is the author of $y \Leftrightarrow x$ wrote y' (which is true provided x is a literary work) and less dependable ones like 'x caused $y \Leftrightarrow y$ is blamed on x'. This work was refined by Pantel *et al.* (2007) by assigning the x and y terms semantic types (*inferential selectional preferences* – ISP) based on lexical abstraction from empirically observed argument types. A limitation of the approach is that the conditional rules obtained are largely limited to ones expressing some rough synonymy or similarity relation. Pekar (2006) developed related methods for learning the implications of an event based on the regular co-occurrence of two verbs within "locally coherent text", acquiring rules like 'x was appointed as y' suggests that 'x became y', but, as in DIRT, we lack information about the types of x and y, and only acquire binary relations.

Girju (2003) applied Hearst's (1998) procedure for finding lexico-syntactic patterns to discover causal relations between nouns, as in 'Earthquakes generate tsunami'. Chklovski and Pantel (2004) used pat-

```
(S < (NP $. (VP < (/,/ $. (S < (VP< (VBG<hoping)< (S< (VP< TO))))))))
(S < (NP $. (VP < ((CC < but) $.. (VP < (AUX < did) < (RB </n['o]t/))))))
(S < (NP $. (VP < (AUX $. (ADJP < (JJ $. ((CC < /(but|yet)/) $. JJ)))))))
(S < (NP $. (VP < (/,/ $. (S < (VP < ((VBG < expecting) $.
                                        (S < (VP < TO)))))))))
```

Figure 1: Examples of TGrep2 patterns for finding parse tree fragments that might be abstracted to inference rules. See Rohde (2001) for an explanation of the syntax.

terns like '*x*-ed by *y*-ing' ('obtained by borrowing') to get co-occurrence data on candidate pairs from the Web. They used these co-occurrence counts to obtain a measure of mutual information between pairs of verbs, and hence to assess the strengths of the relations. A shortcoming of rules obtained in this way is their lack of detailed predicative structure. For inference purposes, it would be insufficient to know that 'crashes cause injuries' without having any idea of what is crashing and who or what is being injured.

Schoenmackers *et al.* (2010) derived first-order Horn clauses from the tuple relations found by TEXTRUNNER (Banko *et al.*, 2007). Their system produces rules like 'IsHeadquarteredIn(Company, State) :- IsBasedIn(Company, City) ∧ IsLocatedIn(City, State)', which are intended to improve inference for question-answering. A limitation of this approach is that, operating on the facts discovered by an information extraction system, it largely obtains relations among simple attributes like locations or roles rather than consequences or reasons.

3 Method

Our method first uses TGrep2 (Rohde, 2001) to find parse trees matching hand-authored lexico-syntactic patterns, centered around certain pragmatically significant cue words such as 'hoping to' or 'but didn't'. Some of the search patterns are in Figure 1. While we currently use eight query patterns, future work may add rules to cover more constructions.

The matched parse trees are filtered to remove those unlikely to produce reasonable results, such as those containing parentheses or quoted utterances, and the trees are preprocessed in a top-down traversal to rewrite or remove constituents that are usually extraneous. For instance, the parse tree for

> *The next day he and another Bengali boy who lives near by* [sic] *chose another way home, hoping to escape the attackers.*

is preprocessed to

> People chose another way home, hoping to escape the attackers.

Examples of the preprocessing rules include removing interjections (INTJ) and some prepositional phrases, heuristically turning long expressions into keywords like 'a proposition', abstracting named entities, and reordering some sentences to be easier to process. *E.g.*, 'Fourteen inches from the floor it's supposed to be' is turned to 'It's supposed to be fourteen inches from the floor'.

The trees are then rewritten as conditional expressions based on which semantic pattern they match, as outlined in the following subsections. The sample sentences are from the Brown Corpus (Kučera and Francis, 1967) and the British National Corpus (BNC Consortium, 2001), and the rules are those derived by our current system.

3.1 Disconfirmed Expectations

These are sentences where 'but' or 'yet' is used to indicate that the expected inference people would make does not hold. In such cases, we want to flip the polarity of the conclusion (adding or removing 'not' from the output) so that the expectation is confirmed. For instance, from

> *The ship weighed anchor and ran out her big guns, but did not fire a shot.*

we get that the normal case is the opposite:

> If a ship weighs anchor and runs out her big guns, then it may fire a shot.

Or for two adjectives, 'She was poor but proud':

> If a female is poor, then she may not be proud.

3.2 Contrasting Good and Bad

A different use of 'but' and 'yet' is to contrast something considered good with something considered bad, as in 'He is very clever but eccentric':

> If a male is very clever,
> then he may be eccentric.

If we were to treat this as a case of disconfirmed expectation as above, we would have claimed that 'If a male is very clever, then he may not be eccentric'. To identify this special use of 'but', we consult a lexicon of sentiment annotations, SentiWordNet (Baccianella *et al.*, 2010). Finding that 'clever' is positive while 'eccentric' is negative, we retain the surface polarity in this case.

For sentences with full sentential complements for 'but', recognizing good and bad items is quite difficult, more often depending on pragmatic information. For instance, in

> *Central government knew this would happen but did not want to admit to it in its plans.*

knowing something is generally good while being unwilling to admit something is bad. At present, we don't deal with these cases.

3.3 Expected Outcomes

Other sentences give us a participant's intent, and we just want to abstract sufficiently to form a general rule:

> *He stood before her in the doorway, evidently expecting to be invited in.*
>
> If a male stands before a female in the doorway, then he may expect to be invited in.

When we abstract from named entities (using a variety of hand-built gazetteers), we aim low in the hierarchy:

> *Elisabeth smiled, hoping to lighten the conversational tone and distract the Colonel from his purpose.*
>
> If a female smiles, then she may hope to lighten the conversational tone.

While most general rules about 'a male' or 'a female' could instead be about 'a person', there are ones that can't, such as those about giving birth. We leave the raising of terms for later work, following Van Durme *et al.* (2009).

4 Evaluation

Development was based on examples from the (hand-parsed) Brown Corpus and the (machine-parsed) British National Corpus, as alluded to above. These corpora were chosen for their broad coverage of everyday situations and edited writing.

As the examples in the preceding subsections indicate, rules extracted by our method often describe complex consequences or reasons, and subtle relations among adjectival attributes, that appear to be quite different from the kinds of rules targeted in previous work (as discussed earlier, or at venues such as that of (Sekine, 2008)). While we would like to evaluate the discovered rules by looking at inferences made with them, that must wait until logical forms are automatically created; here we judge the rules themselves.

> The statement above is a reasonably clear, entirely plausible, generic claim and seems neither too specific nor too general or vague to be useful:
>
> 1. I agree.
> 2. I lean towards agreement.
> 3. I'm not sure.
> 4. I lean towards disagreement.
> 5. I disagree.

Figure 2: Instructions for judging of unsharpened factoids.

Judge 1	*Judge 2*	*Correlation*
1.84	2.45	0.55

Table 1: Average ratings and Pearson correlation for rules from the personal stories corpus. Lower ratings are better; see Fig. 2.

For evaluation, we used a corpus of personal stories from weblogs (Gordon and Swanson, 2009), parsed with a statistical parser (Charniak, 2000). We sampled 100 output rules and rated them on a scale of 1–5 (1 being best) based on the criteria in Fig. 2. To decide if a rule meets the criteria, it is helpful to imagine a dialogue with a computer agent. Told an instantiated form of the antecedent, the agent asks for confirmation of a potential conclusion. *E.g.*, for

> If attacks are brief,
> then they may not be intense,

the dialogue would go:

> "The attacks (on Baghdad) were brief."
> "So I suppose they weren't intense, were they?"

If this is a reasonable follow-up, then the rule is probably good, although we also disprefer very unlikely antecedents – rules that are vacuously true.

As the results in Table 1 and Fig. 3 indicate, the overall quality of the rules learned is good but there is room for improvement. We also see a rather low correlation between the ratings of the two judges, indicating the difficulty of evaluating the quality of the rules, especially since their expression in natural language (NL) makes it tempting to "fill in the blanks" of what we understand them to mean. We hypothesize that the agreement between judges will be higher for rules in logical form, where malformed output is more readily identified – for instance, there is no guessing about coreference or attachment.

Rules that both judges rated favorably (1) include:

> If a pain is great, it may not be manageable.
>
> If a person texts a male, then he-or-she may get a reply.

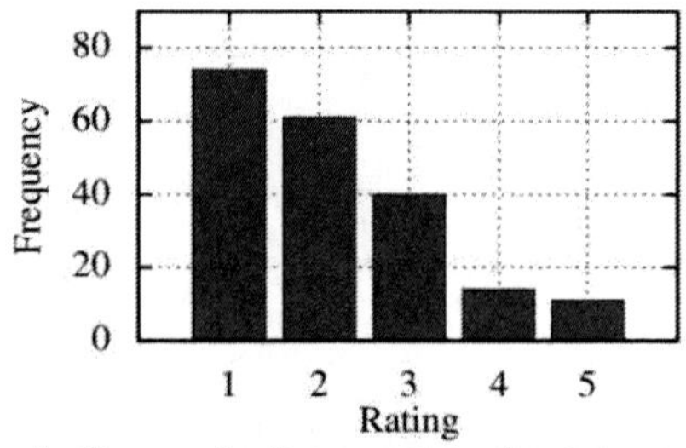

Figure 3: Counts for how many rules were assigned each rating by judges. Lower ratings are better; see Fig. 2.

> If a male looks around, then he may hope to see someone.
>
> If a person doesn't like some particular store, then he-or-she may not keep going to it.

While some bad rules come from parsing or processing mistakes, these are less of a problem than the heavy tail of difficult constructions. For instance, there are idioms that we want to filter out (*e.g.*, 'I'm embarrassed but...') and other bad outputs show context-dependent rather than general relations:

> If a girl sits down in a common room, then she may hope to avoid some pointless conversations.

The sitting-down may not have been *because* she wanted to avoid conversation but because of something prior.

It's difficult to compare our results to other systems because of the differences of representation, types of rules, and evaluation methods. ISP's best performing method (ISP.JIM) achieves 0.88 specificity (defined as a filter's probability of rejecting incorrect inferences) and 0.53 accuracy. While describing their SHERLOCK system, Schoenmackers *et al.* (2010) argue that "the notion of 'rule quality' is vague except in the context of an application" and thus they evaluate the Horn clauses they learn in the context of the HOLMES inference-based QA system, finding that at precision 0.8 their rules allow the system to find twice as many correct facts. Indeed, our weak rater agreement shows the difficulty of judging rules on their own, and future work aims to evaluate rules extrinsically.

5 Conclusion and Future Work

Enabling an inference system to reason about common situations and activities requires more types of general world knowledge and lexical knowledge than are currently available or have been targeted by previous work. We've suggested an initial approach to acquiring rules describing complex consequences or reasons and subtle relations among adjectival attributes: We find possible rules by looking at interesting discourse patterns and rewriting them as conditional expressions based on semantic patterns.

A natural question is why we don't use the machine-learning/bootstrapping techniques that are common in other work on acquiring rules. These techniques are particularly successful when (a) they are aimed at finding fixed types of relationships, such as hyponymy, near-synonymy, part-of, or causal relations between pairs of lexical items (often nominals or verbs); and (b) the fixed type of relationship between the lexical items is hinted at sufficiently often either by their co-occurrence in certain local lexico-syntactic patterns, or by their occurrences in similar sentential environments (distributional similarity). But in our case, (a) we are looking for a broad range of (more or less strong) consequence relationships, and (b) the relationships are between entire clauses, not lexical items. We are simply not likely to find multiple occurrences of the same pair of clauses in a variety of syntactic configurations, all indicating a consequence relation – you're unlikely to find multiple redundant patterns relating clauses, as in 'Went up to the door but didn't knock on it'.

There is more work to be done to arrive at a reliable, inference-ready knowledge base of such rules. The primary desideratum is to produce a logical representation for the rules such that they can be used in the EPILOG reasoner (Schubert and Hwang, 2000). Computing logical forms (as, *e.g.*, in Bos (2008)) and then deriving logically formulated rules from these rather than deriving sentential forms directly from text should also allow us to be more precise about dropping modifiers, reshaping into generic present tense from other tenses, and other issues that affect the quality of the statements. We have a preliminary version of a logical form generator that derives LFs from TreeBank parses that can support this direction. Further filtering techniques (based both on the surface form and the logical form) should keep the desired inference rules while improving quality.

Acknowledgements

This work was supported by NSF grants IIS-1016735 and IIS-0916599, and ONR STTR subcontract N00014-10-M-0297.

References

Stefano Baccianella, Andrea Esuli, and Fabrizio Sebastiani. 2010. SentiWordNet 3.0: An enhanced lexical resource for sentiment analysis and opinion mining. In *Proc. of the Seventh Conference on International Language Resources and Evaluation (LREC'10)*.

Michele Banko, Michael J. Cafarella, Stephen Soderland, Matt Broadhead, and Oren Etzioni. 2007. Open information extraction from the Web. In *Proc. of the Twentieth International Joint Conference on Artificial Intelligence (IJCAI-07)*.

BNC Consortium. 2001. The British National Corpus, v.2. Distributed by Oxford University Computing Services.

Johan Bos. 2008. Wide-coverage semantic analysis with Boxer. In *Proc. of the Symposium on Semantics in Text Processing (STEP 2008)*.

Eugene Charniak. 2000. A maximum-entropy-inspired parser. In *Proc. of the First Annual Meeting of the North American Chapter of the Association for Computational Linguistics (NAACL 2000)*, pages 132–139.

Timothy Chklovski and Patrick Pantel. 2004. VerbOcean: Mining the Web for fine-grained semantic verb relations. In *Proc. of the Conference on Empirical Methods in Natural Language Processing (EMNLP-04)*.

Roxana Girju. 2003. Automatic detection of causal relations for question answering. In *Proc. of the ACL 2003 Workshop on Multilingual Summarization and Question Answering – Machine Learning and Beyond*.

Jonathan Gordon and Lenhart K. Schubert. 2010. Quantificational sharpening of commonsense knowledge. In *Proc. of the AAAI 2010 Fall Symposium on Commonsense Knowledge*.

Andrew Gordon and Reid Swanson. 2009. Identifying personal stories in millions of weblog entries. In *Proc. of the Third International Conference on Weblogs and Social Media (ICWSM), Data Challenge Workshop*.

Marti Hearst. 1998. Automated discovery of WordNet relations. In Christiane Fellbaum, editor, *WordNet: An Electronic Lexical Database and Some of Its Applications*. MIT Press.

Henry Kučera and W. N. Francis. 1967. *Computational Analysis of Present-Day American English*. Brown University Press.

Dekang Lin and Patrick Pantel. 2001. DIRT: Discovery of inference rules from text. In *Proc. of the ACM Conference on Knowledge Discovery and Data Mining (KDD)*.

Patrick Pantel, Rahul Bhagat, Timothy Chklovski, and Eduard Hovy. 2007. ISP: Learning inferential selectional preferences. In *Proc. of NAACL-HLT 2007*.

Viktor Pekar. 2006. Acquisition of verb entailment from text. In *Proc. of HLT-NAACL 2006*.

Doug Rohde. 2001. TGrep2 manual. Unpublished manuscript, Brain & Cognitive Science Department, MIT.

Stefan Schoenmackers, Oren Etzioni, Daniel S. Weld, and Jesse Davis. 2010. Learning first-order horn clauses from Web text. In *Proc. of EMNLP 2010*.

Lenhart K. Schubert and Chung Hee Hwang. 2000. Episodic Logic Meets Little Red Riding Hood: A comprehensive, natural representation for language understanding. In L. Iwanska and S. C. Shapiro, editors, *Natural Language Processing and Knowledge Representation: Language for Knowledge and Knowledge for Language*. MIT/AAAI Press.

Satoshi Sekine, editor. 2008. *Notebook of the NSF Symposium on Semantic Knowledge Discovery, Organization, and Use*. New York University, 14–15 November.

Benjamin Van Durme and Lenhart K. Schubert. 2008. Open knowledge extraction through compositional language processing. In *Proc. of the Symposium on Semantics in Text Processing (STEP 2008)*.

Benjamin Van Durme, Phillip Michalak, and Lenhart K. Schubert. 2009. Deriving Generalized Knowledge from Corpora using WordNet Abstraction. In *Proc. of EACL 2009*.

Author Index

Association for Computational Linguistics
209 N. Eighth Street
Stroudsburg, Pennsylvania 18360

CURRAN ASSOCIATES INC.
proceedings.com